TROUBLE NEXT DOOR:
WHAT TO DO WITH YOUR NEIGHBOR

by
Margaret C. Jasper

Oceana's Legal Almanac Series:
Law for the Layperson

Oceana Publications

You may order this or any other Oxford University Press publication by visiting the Oxford University Press and Oceana websites at www.oup.com and www.oceanalaw.com respectively.

Library of Congress Control Number: 2006935509

ISBN 978-0-19-532366-5

Oceana's Legal Almanac Series: Law for the Layperson
ISSN 1075-7376

©2007 Oxford University Press, Inc.

Manufactured in the United States of America on acid-free paper.

To My Husband Chris

Your love and support
are my motivation and inspiration

-and-

In memory of my son, Jimmy

Table of Contents

CHAPTER 4:
BOUNDARY LINE DISPUTES

CHAPTER 5:
NUISANCE

CHAPTER 6:
PREMISES LIABILITY

CHAPTER 7:
ANIMALS

CHAPTER 8:
ILLEGAL ACTIVITIES

CHAPTER 9:
MEDIATION

CHAPTER 10:
THE LAST RESORT: SMALL CLAIMS COURT

ABOUT THE AUTHOR

MARGARET C. JASPER is an attorney engaged in the general practice of law in South Salem, New York, concentrating in the areas of personal injury and entertainment law. Ms. Jasper holds a Juris Doctor degree from Pacc University School of Law, White Plains, New York, is a member of the New York and Connecticut bars, and is certified to practice before the United States District Courts for the Southern and Eastern Districts of New York, the United States Court of Appeals for the Second Circuit, and the United States Supreme Court.

Ms. Jasper has been appointed to the law guardian panel for the Family Court of the State of New York, is a member of a number of professional organizations and associations, and is a New York State licensed real estate broker operating as Jasper Real Estate in South Salem, New York.

Margaret Jasper maintains a website at http://www.JasperLawOffice.com.

In 2004, Ms. Jasper successfully argued a case before the New York Court of Appeals which gives mothers of babies who are stillborn due to medical negligence the right to bring a legal action and recover emotional distress damages. This successful appeal overturned a 26-year old New York case precedent, which previously prevented mothers of stillborn babies to sue their negligent medical providers.

Ms. Jasper is the author and general editor of the following legal almanacs:

AIDS Law
The Americans with Disabilities Act
Animal Rights Law
Auto Leasing
Bankruptcy Law for the Individual Debtor
Banks and their Customers
Becoming a Citizen
Buying and Selling Your Home

Commercial Law
Consumer Rights Law
Co-ops and Condominiums: Your Rights and Obligations As Owner
Copyright Law
Credit Cards and the Law
Custodial Rights
Dealing with Debt
Dictionary of Selected Legal Terms
Drunk Driving Law
DWI, DUI and the Law
Education Law
Elder Law
Employee Rights in the Workplace
Employment Discrimination Under Title VII
Environmental Law
Estate Planning
Everyday Legal Forms
Executors and Personal Representatives: Rights and
    Responsibilities
Harassment in the Workplace
Health Care and Your Rights
Health Care Directives
Hiring Household Help and Contractors: Your Rights and Obliga-
    tions Under the Law
Home Mortgage Law Primer
Hospital Liability Law
How To Change Your Name
How To Protect Your Challenged Child
How To Start Your Own Business
Identity Theft and How To Protect Yourself
Individual Bankruptcy and Restructuring
Injured on the Job: Employee Rights, Worker's Compensation and
    Disability Insurance Law
International Adoption
Juvenile Justice and Children's Law
Labor Law
Landlord-Tenant Law
Law for the Small Business Owner
The Law of Attachment and Garnishment
The Law of Buying and Selling
The Law of Capital Punishment
The Law of Child Custody
The Law of Contracts
The Law of Debt Collection

The Law of Dispute Resolution
The Law of Immigration
The Law of Libel and Slander
The Law of Medical Malpractice
The Law of No-Fault Insurance
The Law of Obscenity and Pornography
The Law of Personal Injury
The Law of Premises Liability
The Law of Product Liability
The Law of Speech and the First Amendment
The Law of Violence Against Women
Lemon Laws
Living Together: Practical Legal Issues
Living Wills
Marriage and Divorce
Missing and Exploited Children: How to Protect Your Child
Motor Vehicle Law
Nursing Home Negligence
Patent Law
Pet Law
Prescription Drugs
Privacy and the Internet: Your Rights and Expectations Under the Law
Probate Law
Real Estate Law for the Homeowner and Broker
Religion and the Law
Retirement Planning
The Right to Die
Rights of Single Parents
Small Claims Court
Social Security Law
Special Education Law
Teenagers and Substance Abuse
Trademark Law
Trouble Next Door: What to do With Your Neighbor
Victim's Rights Law
Welfare: Your Rights and the Law
What if It Happened to You: Violent Crimes and Victims' Rights
What if the Product Doesn't Work: Warranties & Guarantees
Workers' Compensation Law
Your Child's Legal Rights: An Overview
Your Rights in a Class Action Suit
Your Rights as a Tenant
Your Rights Under the Family and Medical Leave Act
You've Been Fired: Your Rights and Remedies

INTRODUCTION

"Love thy neighbor." Unfortunately, at times, this is easier said than done when you are kept up all night by the sound of your neighbor's dog howling, or when the upstairs neighbor keeps flooding your meticulously kept bathroom by letting their bathtub overflow every week. Even worse situations present themselves when a drug dealer or pedophile decides to move into the neighborhood. There are many scenarios when a neighbor may make you feel less than "neighborly."

This almanac discusses the rights and responsibilities of neighbors, common conflicts, and how to resolve a dispute before it escalates into a costly lawsuit, or worse yet, into violence. This almanac also explores dispute mediation and, as a last resort means to resolve un-neighborly conflicts—e.g. taking your neighbor to small claims court.

The Appendix provides applicable statutes, resource directories, and other pertinent information and data. The Glossary contains definitions of many of the terms used throughout the almanac.

CHAPTER 1:
SOLVING NEIGHBOR PROBLEMS

WHAT IS A NEIGHBOR?

A "neighbor" is generally defined as "somebody who lives or is located very close by"—the key word being "close." If you live in a house, your neighbor is the person who lives next door, or on the same street. If you live in an apartment, your neighbor is the person who lives in a nearby apartment. Thus, unless you live on a farm in a rural area, or on a large estate surrounded by acres of land, you will likely have one or more "neighbors."

The word "neighborly" is generally defined as "friendly, helpful and kind, especially to a neighbor." Unfortunately, not all neighbors are neighborly. This almanac discusses the various problems you may encounter living with your neighbors, and how best to handle those problems.

THE CONCILIATORY APPROACH

Before you take any formal action, such as notifying the authorities or bringing a lawsuit against your neighbor, you should try to discuss the problem first. It is possible that your neighbor did not realize their activities were disturbing you. If your neighbor becomes hostile, and refuses to listen, your next step would be to put them on notice about the problem, in writing.

If there is a local ordinance that prohibits your neighbor's activities, attach a copy of the law to your letter so that your neighbor is aware that he or she is not merely annoying you, but violating the law as well.

A sample warning letter is set forth at Appendix 1 of this almanac.

If your neighbor disagrees with your position, you can suggest working the problem out with a mediator—an impartial third person—before contacting the authorities or going to court.

Mediation is discussed in Chapter 9 of this almanac.

If your neighbor will not voluntarily work with you to resolve the problem, and refuses to mediate the problem, you may have no alternative but to report their activities to the proper enforcement authorities and/or file a private lawsuit against your neighbor, as discussed below.

WHO DO YOU CALL?

If you have to contact the authorities to make a complaint about your neighbor, you must first determine who to contact to help resolve the matter. This largely depends on the type of problem you are having with your neighbor. You should familiarize yourself with the local laws to find out if there is a specific rule or regulation that governs a specific problem.

If the activity is covered by a law, you should contact the authority responsible for enforcing that law. If, however, the problem or activity you are having with your neighbor is not covered by any specific rule or regulation, you may have no other recourse but to take your neighbor to court and sue on the basis that your neighbor is unreasonably interfering with your use and enjoyment of your property.

Zoning Violations

If your problem involves a dispute over the height of a fence, a boundary line dispute, or your neighbor using his garage as a mechanic's bay, your rights would likely be defined in the local government's zoning regulations. Zoning refers to the approved use of a particular piece of property. Zoning regulations generally govern fence height restrictions, the use of residential property for commercial purposes, and many other zoning-related issues.

Ordinarily, government officials do not become aware of a problem unless someone complains, therefore, don't expect them to come out and investigate on their own. If you believe your neighbor may be violating a zoning ordinance, you can go to the library to review the law or call your local government office or zoning board to find out if there is a regulation that applies to your neighbor's activity. If so, you can file a complaint and ask the appropriate authorities to enforce the law.

If your neighbor is found to have violated a zoning ordinance, he or she will be ordered to stop the offending activities and/or pay a fine. However, you will not be able to recover any monetary compensation for losses sustained by your neighbor's actions unless you personally file a lawsuit to recover damages.

Nuisance Complaints

If your neighbor harbors a menacing dog that chases you every time you leave your front door, habitually leaves trash around the property, or conducts dangerous experiments in the backyard, these activities could be categorized as common-law nuisance and your recourse would be to contact the appropriate agency. Nuisance is generally defined as an unreasonable action by a person that interferes with your enjoyment of your property.

When evaluating a nuisance complaint, the authorities will require the complaint to be reasonable. You can't complain about every little thing you dislike about your neighbor's activities. You may not like the way they decorate their home, or the color they painted their front door, however, this would not rise to the level of nuisance.

If nuisance is considered a civil violation under the law of your jurisdiction, and your neighbor is found guilty, he or she may receive a fine. If nuisance is considered a crime—usually a misdemeanor—under the law of your jurisdiction, your neighbor will be given a summons to appear in court, and may be fined or jailed if convicted. Either way, the government has the burden of prosecution, and you will testify at the trial as a witness to the incident. You will not receive any compensation for losses sustained as a result of your neighbor's actions unless you also take them to court in a private lawsuit.

Depending on the specific activity, the problem may not be covered under the local zoning law. For example, if you have neighbors that are constantly and loudly arguing in their backyard, or their three boys are continually straddling the boundary fence, screaming loudly, and driving your dogs crazy, this may negatively affect your enjoyment of your property. Nevertheless, their behavior may not be covered under any particular statute other than a potential noise or trespass violation, which would be quite subjective.

In that case, your only recourse may be to file a private nuisance lawsuit against your neighbor and request a court order requiring your neighbor to end the offensive activity. You may also seek monetary compensation for any losses you have suffered as a result of their activities. Generally, you would file your lawsuit in small claims court, which is less costly than going to a higher court and doesn't require the expertise of an attorney because the proceedings are designed to be informal.

In order to prevail in your lawsuit, you basically have to show that your neighbor's activities are offensive, that you have tried to get your neighbor to voluntarily comply with your request, that your neighbor's actions have negatively impacted your ability to use and enjoy your property, and that you are entitled to monetary compensation and/or an injunction requiring your neighbor to stop the offensive activities.

The process of filing a lawsuit in small claims court is discussed in Chapter 10 of this almanac.

Neighborhood Crime

If the problem you are concerned about deals with a crime, such as a drug dealer living next door, vandalism, or a suspected pedophile in the neighborhood, you should contact your local law enforcement authorities immediately.

CO-TENANTS AND LANDLORD LIABILITY

If you live in an apartment building, your problem with a neighbor will likely be magnified as you are all basically living under the same roof. You probably use the same incinerator room to dispose of trash, and your shared walls are certainly no barrier to everyday noise much less loud music. Of course, by choosing to live in an apartment building, your expectations of privacy and "quiet" enjoyment of the premises are somewhat reduced, however, you are still entitled to a reasonable degree of civility from your neighbors.

Your landlord would not be responsible for the actions of the co-tenants living in the apartment building unless the landlord either expressly or impliedly authorized any action by a co-tenant which would intrude upon your enjoyment of the property. For example, the landlord is generally not responsible because a tenant in the apartment building plays loud music at all hours of the day and night, disturbing neighboring tenants.

Thus, if you have a problem with your neighbor, and you cannot convince the offending tenant to cooperate, e.g., by playing music at a reasonable level and during reasonable hours of the day, you should file a written complaint with the landlord. If a number of tenants join in the complaint, the landlord will likely advise the offending tenant to quiet down or face eviction. If the landlord fails to take any action to reduce the noise or other problem after being put on notice, he or she may then be held liable for a breach of the covenant of quiet enjoyment of the leased premises.

Landlords are also required to be vigilant about tenant crime, and most states hold landlords legally responsible to some degree for protecting their tenants from the criminal actions of co-tenants and employees.

For example, the landlord may be held legally responsible for tenants who deal drugs from their apartments, particularly if it can be shown that the landlord knew about the situation and failed to take any action against the tenant. Landlords must be aware of activities taking place on the rental property, and take swift action if a problem arises.

Therefore, your first course of action when dealing with a co-tenant problem, if you cannot get the tenant to cooperate voluntarily, would be to contact the landlord and file a formal complaint. If your landlord fails to take action after being put on notice, you can take the landlord and your neighbor to court and sue for damages and an order requiring your neighbor to stop the activities.

CONDOMINIUMS, CO-OPS AND PLANNED DEVELOPMENTS

Residents of condominium, cooperative or planned developments are usually subject to private rules and regulations governed by a home-owners' association, co-op board, or similar governing board. These organizations exercise a lot of control over people living within the community. The deeds to houses in new developments usually include limitations on how the property can be used. These rules are referred to as covenants, conditions, and restrictions (CC&Rs), and they are usually quite detailed. The development may also have bylaws and other regulations that prohibit the offending activity.

The regulations of a planned development are designed to increase the value of the homes in the development; therefore, enforcement of the rules tends to be rather strict. The rules commonly limit the landscaping around the home, the color of the house, and even the color of any blinds or curtains that are visible from the front. Uniformity is the goal.

Basically, any problem you may encounter with your neighbor that involves upkeep of their property, noise, boundary disputes, fencing, pets, hazardous conditions, home businesses, view obstruction, crime, etc., will be governed by the rules and regulations of the development, and your complaint should be made directly to the governing body. If a resident violates these rules, they may be fined or otherwise penalized, and failure to comply may lead to proceedings to force their removal from the development.

A sample condominium fine policy is set forth at Appendix 2 of this almanac.

CHAPTER 2:
FENCES

IN GENERAL

"Good fences make good neighbors." The key word in this saying is "good." Fences have led to many arguments between neighbors. The fence may be in disrepair, an unsightly color, too high, or encroach on another's property. The question is what—if anything—can you do about it? As with any dispute between neighbors, you must consider whether you can live with the problem fence, or whether it so disturbs you that you'll risk making an enemy who lives next door.

FENCE HEIGHT

A fence may be artificial or natural. An artificial fence is a constructed fence, e.g., a wood picket fence, a chain link fence, etc. A natural fence is one that is formed by trees or bushes. In most residential areas, an artificial backyard fence cannot exceed six feet and a front yard fence cannot exceed four feet. Depending on the local rules, there may also be height restrictions for natural fences. Before you speak with your neighbor, you should obtain a copy of the local fence height regulation from your building department.

A sample fence height ordinance is set forth at Appendix 3 of this almanac.

Before you report your neighbor's fence height violation to the local authorities, you should speak with him or her to see whether they will voluntarily agree to your request for compliance with the zoning ordinance. It is possible that they aren't even aware of the fence height restriction. Bring a copy of the regulation with you when you meet with your neighbor.

You should amicably point out how their fence violates the local regulations and why you are opposed to the height of the fence. If the fence is still being built, you may be able to get your neighbor to change their plans to conform to the height restriction. If they refuse to make changes, you can more adamantly advise them that you will have no recourse but to notify the local authorities. If they still refuse to comply, you have no choice but to report the violation. The town will likely order your neighbor to follow the law or risk a fine or other penalty.

Nevertheless, if the town does not take action against your neighbor for the fence violation, you have two options. If you will be satisfied with a monetary settlement, you can take your neighbor to small claims court, alleging that the fence has caused you to lose enjoyment of your property, e.g., it obstructed your view. If you prevail, you may receive compensation, however, the fence will remain in place insofar as a small claims court may not be able to issue an order requiring the owner to remove the fence. Small claims courts are informal and designed for individuals to bring claims without the necessity of hiring an attorney.

The process of bringing a small claims case is discussed in Chapter 10 of this almanac.

If you absolutely cannot live with the fence and want it taken down, you may have to go to trial court and ask a judge to order removal of the fence. However, you will probably have to hire a lawyer to represent you, as the procedures are more complex in higher courts than in small claims court.

GRANDFATHER CLAUSE

A grandfather clause basically means that a condition that would be unlawful or prohibited under a new law will not apply if the condition pre-dated the law. As it pertains to fences, a grandfather clause would allow a fence that violates a height restriction to remain because it was in existence prior to the law prohibiting such a fence.

For example, if there is an 8-foot fence separating your property from your neighbor's property, and the fence was put up before there was a height restriction, you may not succeed in challenging the legality of your neighbor's fence if it was subject to a grandfather clause. Nevertheless, if your neighbor tears down that fence, he or she cannot erect another 8-foot fence in its place, and any new fence would have to conform to the height restriction.

OBTAINING A VARIANCE

You may want to erect a fence that violates a local zoning ordinance, such as a height restriction, for good cause, e.g., to limit traffic noise from an adjacent highway. In order to do so, you need permission—known as a "variance"—from your local government. A variance, if granted, permits you to depart from local zoning laws and use your land in a manner not ordinarily permitted by the zoning ordinance.

After applying for a variance, you will generally be required to post a notice on your property advising your neighbors that you are seeking the variance. You may also be required to publish your request for a variance in a local newspaper. At some point, a hearing will be scheduled where neighbors can voice their objections to your request. The governing authority—e.g., the zoning board—will make a decision and, if it determines your request is justified, will issue the variance. You can then legally build the fence and you do not have to worry about someone suing you in court to remove it.

CONDOMINIUMS, CO-OPS AND PLANNED DEVELOPMENTS

If you live in a condominium, co-op or planned development, there are usually restrictions on the type of fence you can erect, the materials you can use to build the fence, and the maximum height of the fence. The concern is that there is conformity among the homes located in the community.

If you move into a home in a planned community, you are obligated to follow these rules. The restriction may be written in your deed, the by-laws, or may be spelled out in a separate document known as the Covenants, Conditions and Restrictions (CC&Rs).

If you deviate from the restrictions, the homeowner's association will generally issue warnings requesting you to comply with the rules. If you ignore the warnings, the homeowner's association can assess penalties against you, and sue you in court to force your compliance.

FENCE APPEARANCE

An unsightly border fence may be difficult to look at, however, it usually doesn't violate any local ordinance as long as it is not a safety hazard, e.g., if it is topped with barbed wire. There may be some local restrictions; therefore, you should check the local zoning laws. For example, some towns require that the posts, and/or unfinished areas of a fence face the property of the person who is building the fence:

VILLAGE OF MASSAPEQUA

ZONING LAW

§345-40 (C) Location of posts and unfinished side facings.

Any fence constructed in accordance with this section shall have the fence posts and/or unfinished side facings and/or horizontal and diagonal cross member pieces facing inward and located on the inside and/or that side of the property of the person who is erecting said fence. In the event that there is any question in reference to the above, it shall always be construed in favor of the adjoining property owner and against the person who is erecting said fence as to the location of said fence posts and/or unfinished side facings and/or horizontal and diagonal cross member pieces of the fence and/or any other item relating to the fence.

If the fence is in serious disrepair, and your neighbor refuses to fix it, depending on the law of your jurisdiction, you may be able to have it repaired and sue your neighbor for the cost of the repair.

VIEW OBSTRUCTION

In general, there is no right to a view, air or light, unless a law, rule or regulation guarantees this right. If your home has a scenic view that adds value to the property, you may want to enter into an agreement with your neighbor for an easement to protect your view. The agreement would basically prevent your neighbor from erecting a fence or planting trees that would interfere with your view.

Thus, unless you live in a community that has a view ordinance, you are unlikely to prevail in a lawsuit without such an agreement. An exception may exist if you can demonstrate that your neighbor put the fence up with the intent to maliciously block your view, as this may constitute a spite fence, as further discussed below.

SPITE FENCE

The term "spite fence" refers to fences that are erected for the sole purpose of harassing a neighbor. Generally, such fences have no use to the person erecting them other than spite. The fence may violate local height or appearance regulations. In addition, there may be a law that specifically bans a fence built solely for spite. Therefore, the reader is advised to check the law of his or her own jurisdiction concerning spite fences.

Under certain circumstances, you may be able to sue your neighbor to have the fence taken down if you can prove your neighbor built the fence with malicious intent for no reason other than to aggravate you.

You may also recover compensation for the diminished value of your property caused by the erection and maintenance of the spite fence.

Rhode Island's "spite fence" statute states as follows:

R.I. GENERAL LAWS

§ 34-10-20 Spite fences.—

A fence or other structure in the nature of a fence which unnecessarily exceeds six feet (6') in height and is maliciously erected or maintained for the purpose of annoying the owners or occupants of adjoining property, shall be deemed a private nuisance, and any owner or occupant who is injured, either in the comfort or enjoyment of his or her estate thereby, may have an action to recover damages for the injury.

BOUNDARY FENCES

In general, if you build and use a fence that sits on the boundary line between your property and your neighbor's property, you would be deemed the owner of the fence. However, if your neighbor uses the fence as his or her own, it may be considered a "boundary fence" co-owned by you and your neighbor. In that case, both you and your neighbor are responsible for the cost of repair and maintenance of the boundary fence.

Disagreement over cost-sharing commonly leads to a dispute. For example, you may want to paint the fence, but your neighbor doesn't agree that it needs to be painted and refuses to chip in on the cost. If your desire to paint the fence is merely a personal preference, your neighbor shouldn't have to share in the cost of painting at your whim. However, if the fence needs to be painted because it is chipping and peeling so much that it is negatively affecting the property values, your neighbor is required to share the cost.

After you have pointed out the problem to your neighbor, you should follow up with a letter requesting their contribution towards cost of repair or maintenance.

A cost-sharing request letter is set forth at Appendix 4 of this almanac.

If you cannot get your neighbor to agree to share the costs of repair and maintenance of a boundary fence, you may go ahead and make the necessary repairs and then seek reimbursement from your neighbor for his or her share of the costs. However, before having the fence fixed, you should take pictures so that you have proof of its condition should you end up in court. In addition, obtain one or two additional estimates for repair so that you will be able to demonstrate to the court that the costs you are seeking are reasonable.

After the repair has been completed, you should send your neighbor a letter demanding reimbursement for their share of the repair cost.

A demand for reimbursement is set forth at Appendix 5 of this almanac.

If your neighbor still refuses to reimburse you, you may have no choice but to take him or her to small claims court and sue for reimbursement. You should bring all of the documentation you have gathered, including your letters to your neighbor, the pictures, the estimates, and the paid bill. This will serve as evidence of your attempt to be resolve the issue, the necessity of the repair, and the reasonableness of the amount sought. In some states, if your neighbor refuses to chip in, depending on the state statute, he or she could be required to pay you double the cost of repair or maintenance.

Before you take your neighbor to court, you should first make sure the fence is indeed a "boundary fence." The key factor in determining whether the fence is a boundary fence is "use" of the fence. If the fence just sits there on the boundary line, and your neighbor has no contact with it whatsoever, it is unlikely the fence would be considered a boundary fence. However, if your neighbor takes certain actions, this could create a boundary fence.

For example, if your neighbor joins another fence to your fence, e.g., to enclose his or her own property, this could be interpreted as creating a boundary fence, and he or she would be equally responsible for repair and maintenance of the fence, absent an agreement to the contrary.

If one neighbor uses an existing fence to enclose his or her own property, most state laws require some compensation to the fence owner for the benefit of using the existing fence. He or she would then be considered a co-owner of the fence. Nevertheless, although the law requiring compensation for fence joining may be on the books, as a practical matter, most neighbors do not seek to enforce it.

If you and your neighbor do not want to share ownership of a boundary fence, you can agree that only one of you will be responsible for the fence, or that one of you will be more responsible for the fence than the other. In most states, if your neighbor later sells their property, the new owner is not bound by the agreement. You will need to obtain a whole new agreement with the new neighbor. However, a small minority of states permit you to record the agreement with the county clerk, and bind heirs and assigns—i.e., anyone who later acquires an interest in the property—to the agreement.

For example, Vermont's statute provides as follows:

VERMONT STATUTES

TITLE 24: MUNICIPAL AND COUNTY GOVERNMENT

CHAPTER 109: FENCES AND FENCE VIEWERS

§ 3812. Agreement as to Division

An agreement in writing between the owners of adjoining lands, relating to their division fence, signed by the owners, witnessed by two witnesses, acknowledged by the parties and recorded in the office of the town clerk in the town where the fence is situated shall be valid against the parties, their heirs and assigns.

USING FENCE VIEWERS TO RESOLVE DISPUTES

When faced with a dispute between neighbors, many states have "fence viewer" statutes to assist in resolving the problem. A fence viewer is an individual who is appointed to inspect the fence that is the subject of the dispute, and to make a decision as to the amount, if any, one neighbor owes the other. If the fence viewer agrees that the fence needed repair, the non-paying neighbor will be required to contribute to the cost or risk a fine for noncompliance. The fence viewer's decision is binding, however, it can be appealed in court.

A sample fence viewer statute is set forth at Appendix 6 of this almanac.

CHAPTER 3:
TREES

IN GENERAL

Another area of conflict between neighbors often involves trees. For example, tree branches may hang over your property, or the roots may grow under your property. Trees that are not properly maintained may damage your property or injure someone. Before you approach your neighbor about a tree problem, you should first determine ownership of the tree.

Under the law, if the trunk of the tree is solely on your neighbor's property, then the tree belongs to your neighbor. If the tree trunk is situated partly on your neighbor's land and partly on your land, it is called a boundary tree and likely belongs to both you and your neighbor. If the tree is a boundary tree, both you and your neighbor are responsible for taking care of the tree, and neither you nor your neighbor can take the tree out without the other's permission. Generally, the owner of the tree is entitled to compensation and has the right to sue for damages if anyone removes or otherwise hurts a tree without their permission.

OVERHANGING BRANCHES

The trunk of your neighbor's tree may be on his or her property, but the tree may have grown so tall and wide that its branches hang over your property. This may lead to branches, leaves, and other foliage landing on your property, ending up in your pool, etc., causing a big mess that has to be cleaned up.

You are generally permitted to trim any branches of your neighbor's tree that hang over the property line, although you cannot do anything that will harm the tree itself. If you do so intentionally, you will be liable to your neighbor for damages, e.g., the value of the tree and related costs, such as the cost of removing the dead tree from the property. Likewise, if your neighbor harms a tree on your property, you can sue for compensation. In addition, you cannot enter your neighbor's yard to trim the tree from the other side of the property line.

ROOT DAMAGE

Sometimes the neighbor's tree can find its way under your property, as its roots grow and can extend many feet out from the trunk of the tree. Liability for damages caused by the spreading roots of your neighbor's tree depends on your local law. Usually, you cannot sue your neighbor because the roots of his or her tree spread under your property, causing damage to your property, although you may be entitled to trim back the roots of the tree. Some states allow you to sue your neighbor for damages under certain circumstances, e.g., if the roots cause serious harm to your property. Serious harm may include structural damage to your property, e.g., damage to walls, the underground well, the septic system, etc.

HAZARDOUS TREES

A tree may also present a danger if it is unstable. A very large tree can cause considerable damage to your home and injury to anyone in its path should it fall, either because it is a dying, weak tree, or due to a big storm. Under the law, trees that have been planted by abutting property owners are the maintenance responsibility of the current abutting property owner. Likewise, it is your responsibility to provide for the safety of trees on your property.

If the owner of the tree refuses to have the tree evaluated or remove the dangerous tree, you should contact your local authorities, who will likely require your neighbor to take care of the dangerous tree. Many local ordinances prohibit any dangerous condition on private property, including a hazardous tree. If the owner of the tree refuses to comply, he or she may be fined and/or ordered to remove the tree from their property.

Without any special knowledge or abilities when it comes to trees, the average person cannot usually judge the frailty of a tree simply by looking at it from the outside. You would need an arborist—an expert in the cultivation and care of trees—to make the determination as to whether a tree presents a hazard. According to the International Society of Arboriculture (ISA), some defects to look for that could cause problems include the following:

1. Dead Wood—Dead trees and large dead branches are unpredictable. Dead wood is brittle, and cannot bend in the wind like a living tree or branch.

2. Cracks—A crack is a deep split in the tree, which extends through the bark and into the wood of the tree. Cracks are indicators of potential branch or tree failure.

3. Decay—A "hollow" tree can be prone to failure, but presence of decay does not necessarily indicate that the tree is hazardous. Trees usually decay from the inside, forming a cavity. At the same time, new wood is added to the outside of the tree as it grows. If the outer shell is sound, the tree may be relatively safe. Evaluating the safety of a decaying tree is best left to a trained arborist.

4. Root Problems—Trees with damaged roots may blow over in windstorms. The tree should be checked if: (1) over half of the roots have been crushed or cut; (2) the tree is starting to lean and soil is "pushing up" around the base of the tree on the side opposite the lean; or (3) decay is present in the buttress roots or base of the tree.

5. Poor Tree Composition—An example of poor tree composition would be a tree with a weak branch attachment, a large branch that is out of proportion with the rest of the tree, or a tree that leans excessively.

Nevertheless, evaluating the seriousness of a tree defect is best done by a professional arborist. Once the hazard is recognized, steps may be taken to reduce the likelihood of the tree falling and injuring someone or damaging property. The ISA certifies professionals to inspect trees for defects and weakness in branches that otherwise may go unnoticed. For further information, you can contact the ISA as follows:

International Society of Arboriculture
1400 West Anthony Drive
Champaign, IL 61821
Phone: 217.355.9411
Fax: 217.355.9516
E-mail: isa@isa-arbor.com
Website: www.isa-arbor.com

NATURAL DISASTERS

If your neighbor's tree falls on your home during a severe thunderstorm, damaging your roof, you generally have to prove the neighbor negligently maintained the tree in order to recover damages. If the tree was a healthy, well-maintained tree, and the damage was caused by an "act of God," your neighbor will probably not be responsible for the damage. If your neighbor was careless—e.g., he or she knew that the tree was in a state of serious decay and failed to remove it—you will likely be able to recover damages.

CHAPTER 4:
BOUNDARY LINE DISPUTES

IN GENERAL

Disputes concerning boundary lines are not as common as the other problems neighbors face, largely due to surveys that clearly define real property, as further discussed below. The survey includes a legal description of your property that is contained in your deed.

Occasionally, however, a question may arise concerning a property description contained in a deed recorded long ago. This may occur because earlier property descriptions often used natural landmarks to define the property boundaries—e.g., an old oak tree that has since been cut down, or a stream that dried up decades earlier.

If you and your neighbor want to clearly define the boundary lines between your properties, and the legal description is unclear, you have several options:

1. You can agree to the boundary line and issue quitclaim deeds to each other that define the boundary line and grant each other title to the land on either side of that boundary line. The deeds should be recorded with the county clerk.

2. You can hire a surveyor to create a survey of your property, as more fully discussed below.

3. You can go to court and ask a judge to determine the boundary lines.

If you go to court, the judge will likely require you to obtain a survey to assist the court in making the determination, therefore, the only reason to go to court if you have already obtained a survey would be if your neighbor challenges the findings of your surveyor.

THE SURVEY

A survey is a document that shows the location of a piece of property. Boundaries of the property are determined by the survey. A survey assists the property owner in determining whether fences, trees or other such objects are properly located within the property.

If you want an accurate survey of your property, you should contact a professional surveyor. Professional surveyors are often called upon to settle boundary line disputes. Without a properly prepared survey, you may find that you and your neighbor were ignorant of the actual boundary line between your properties.

THE LEGAL DESCRIPTION

As set forth above, your deed contains a legal description of your property. The legal description is based on a detailed survey of the property. It is important that the description be as accurate as possible so that the parties understand exactly what is being conveyed.

There are three common types of legal descriptions used: (1) metes and bounds; (2) record plat; and (3) rectangular.

The Metes and Bounds Survey System

Metes and bounds is a method of describing real property. The metes and bounds survey system is the oldest and most direct method for describing land. Legal descriptions of properties were historically recorded in terms of "metes and bounds" by the settling colonies, hence the archaic language used in the description. "Metes" refers to the actual measurement of the property, and "bounds" refers to the physical boundaries of the property.

The metes and bounds survey system uses physical features of the local geography, along with directions and distances, to define and describe the boundaries of a parcel of land. To survey by metes and bounds, the surveyor describes the boundaries of the property by detailing the direction of, and the distance between, physical points of reference, beginning and ending at the same point. There may be permanent markers placed on the ground, such as metal pipes, where there are no suitable natural landmarks—e.g., trees, streams, etc.—to define the boundaries.

A sample metes and bounds property description is set forth at Appendix 7 of this almanac.

Record Plat Description

The record plat description refers to the method of describing the property by lot and block, also incorporating the existing method of legal description into the detailed record plat.

The Rectangular System

The rectangular system was adopted by Congress in 1785. This is the method used by the majority of states. The rectangular system uses a grid with lines running north and south—known as meridians—and lines running east and west—known as parallels. These lines create squares, each of which represents a certain distance within the town. The squares are divided and subdivided until the land within each section is identified.

KNOW YOUR BOUNDARIES

If you plan to put up a fence, or your neighbor is erecting a fence, consult your survey to make sure you know where the boundary line is located. If you accidentally place the fence on your neighbor's property, he or she can sue you for trespass, and recover money damages. In addition, you will probably have to remove the fence. The same goes if your neighbor accidentally places their fence on your property.

Therefore, if your neighbor starts putting up a fence, and you suspect it is encroaching on your property, ask your neighbor to stop work until you both can verify the exact placement of the fence. In any event, do not permit the fence to go up if it is on any part of your property.

You may not see the harm in having your neighbor's fence extend slightly onto your property, however, as further discussed below, you could risk permanently losing that portion of your property under the adverse possession doctrine, if you fail to take action. If your neighbor refuses to move the fence, you may have to take your neighbor to court.

If you and your neighbor reach an agreement permitting the fence to encroach on your property, the agreement should be put in writing in order to protect your interests. The agreement should plainly state that you are permitting your neighbor to use a portion of your property, but that you are not conveying any portion of your land to your neighbor by allowing them to place the fence on your property.

Nevertheless, this agreement does not bind future owners of the property. If, however, you agree to convey the strip of land to your neighbor, this would be considered a sale of real property, which must be in writing and recorded with the county clerk's office. Such a conveyance would legally change the boundary line of the two properties, and would be binding on any future purchasers.

ADVERSE POSSESSION

It is important to know the boundary lines of your property. Under the adverse possession doctrine, your neighbor may be able to claim ownership rights over a portion of your property provided certain conditions have been met.

Adverse possession is defined as the acquisition of land over the rights of all other persons, including the recorded landowner, by one who has openly, exclusively and continuously possessed the land for a statutory period of time. Depending on the state, this could range from a few short years to as long as twenty-one years. If the record owner, or other interested person, does not come forward within the required time period, title to the property goes to the possessor of the land.

As set forth above, acquisition of land by adverse possession may occur when there has been an encroachment upon neighboring land—e.g., if John Doe builds a fence around his property approximately two feet beyond his property line into Mary Smith's land. This would be an open and obvious encroachment upon Mary Smith's land. If this fence is permitted to remain upon the land for the statutory period of time, John Doe may be able to claim title to the encroached property under the doctrine of adverse possession.

As an example, the Pennsylvania adverse possession statute is set forth at Appendix 8 of this almanac.

CHAPTER 5:
NUISANCE

WHAT IS NUISANCE?

Nuisance is basically defined as a substantial interference with one's right to use and enjoy their land. The interference may be intentional or negligent, and may be public or private. A public nuisance affects the health, safety, or welfare of the public in general. A private nuisance means there has been a loss of the use or enjoyment of property, and can only be asserted by the person who occupies the property. This chapter is concerned with circumstances that constitute private nuisance.

NOISE

Complaints about noisy neighbors are very common. The noise may be caused by boisterous children, loud music, barking dogs, late-night parties, arguments, and a host of other reasons. Whatever the source, noise can be a major headache for the neighbor who is trying to watch television, read a book, or get some sleep.

When determining whether your exposure to noise is actionable, you must consider the circumstances and whether your complaint is reasonable. If you live in an apartment building, you certainly have a lower expectation of solitude, and the noise caused by children running and playing during daytime hours may require a certain amount of tolerance on your part, even if you work at night and sleep during the day. However, if your neighbor's rock band practices at 3 o'clock in the morning in the garage next door, you likely have a legitimate grievance.

The Direct Approach

Your first step in resolving a noise problem is to speak with your neighbor directly. It is possible that your neighbor is not aware of the disturbance they are creating, and may be willing to modify their behavior, e.g., by turning off the stereo by 9 p.m.

If your neighbor ignores your request to keep the noise down, send a warning letter with a copy of your local noise ordinance, and repeat your request that he or she comply with the law.

Apartment Dwellers

If you live in an apartment building, and speaking with your neighbor did not resolve the problem, you should contact the landlord about the noise problem. Most leases have a clause entitling a tenant to "quiet peaceful enjoyment" of the leased premises. Advise the landlord that he or she is responsible for enforcing the terms of your lease, including the covenant of quiet enjoyment.

A sample Covenant of Quiet Enjoyment of Leased Premises is set forth at Appendix 9 of this almanac.

The landlord has the right and power to evict a noisy tenant. If the landlord ignores your request, you can speak with your co-tenants to find out whether they are also disturbed by the problem tenant's noise. There is strength in numbers, and together you may be able to force the landlord to take care of the problem.

If your landlord refuses to take any action, the tenants can put their demand in writing and give the landlord a deadline within which to comply with the duty to ensure the tenants are provided reasonably quiet and peaceful premises. Provide the landlord with all of the details concerning the problem, and ask what he or she plans to do to remedy the situation.

If the landlord continues to ignore the problem after being given written notice, you can notify the landlord of your intention to terminate your lease and move out on the grounds that the apartment is not reasonably fit and habitable due to the noise. If you do not want to terminate your lease, you can advise your landlord that you are going to reduce the rent to reflect the reduction in value of your leased premises. If all of the tenants join in this effort, this would likely motivate the landlord to take action against the noisy neighbor.

Contact the Authorities

If speaking with your neighbor about the noise does not result in any changes in their behavior, or your neighbor becomes hostile, you may have to contact the police, who can issue a warning or arrest your neighbor for disturbing the peace. Call the police at the time the disturbance is occurring, e.g., when the band is blasting their music from the garage next door. Ask for a copy of the police report to document your complaint in case you need to take your neighbor to court for an injunction.

If the police respond to your call, but are reluctant to take any action—e.g., they may love rock music and just do not hear the noise problem you are hearing—you can ask your neighbor whether they will agree to mediation, as discussed in Chapter 9 of this almanac. However, if your neighbor already ignored you when you first tried to discuss the problem, it is unlikely they will agree to mediation. Your only option at this point would be to take your neighbor to small claims court, as discussed in Chapter 10 of this almanac.

Document the Noise Problem

In order to prepare for mediation or litigation, you should document the noise problem. Otherwise, you and your neighbor will be pointing the finger at each other without anything to back up your claim. Keep a journal that details dates, time of day, and what occurred at that time and, if possible, tape-record the noisy activities. Find any witnesses that can back up your story.

Check Your Local Laws

You should also check your local laws to find out if there are any laws relating to noise. Most municipalities have ordinances prohibiting excessive noise to a given number of decibels during certain times of day.

A sample noise ordinance is set forth at Appendix 10.

The police generally have equipment designed to measure the decibel level. If so, ask them to measure the noise coming from your neighbor's home so you can further document your complaint if you proceed to court.

Time Restriction

The typical noise ordinance contains restrictions on noise levels starting at about 10:00 p.m. until 7:00 a.m. on weekdays, and a little later on weekend mornings. The City of Malibu, California has a typical ordinance:

THE NOISE CONTROL ORDINANCE OF THE CITY OF MALIBU

ARTICLE IV: PUBLIC PEACE

CHAPTER 2: NOISE

§ 4204. Prohibited Acts.

Notwithstanding any other provisions of this Chapter, the following acts and the causing or permitting thereof, are declared to be in violation of this Chapter:

B. Radios, Phonographs, Etc. The using, operating or permitting to be played, used or operated between the hours of 10:00 p.m. and 7:00 a.m. of any radio, musical instrument, phonograph, television set, or instrument or device similar to those heretofore specifically mentioned for the production or reproduction of sound in volume sufficiently loud as to disturb the peace, quiet or repose of persons of ordinary and normal sensitiveness who are in the immediate vicinity of such machine or device.

C. Band or Orchestral Rehearsals. The conducting of or carrying on of band or orchestral concerts or rehearsals or practice between the hours of 10:00 p.m. and 7:00 a.m. sufficiently loud as to disturb the peace, quiet or repose of persons of ordinary and normal sensitiveness who reside in the immediate vicinity of such band or orchestral concerts or rehearsals or practice.

Excessive or Unreasonable Noise

Excessive or unreasonable noises may constitute a nuisance at any time of day or night. The City of Atlanta, Georgia has a typical ordinance:

CODE OF ORDINANCES: CITY OF ATLANTA, GEORGIA

PART II CODE OF ORDINANCES—GENERAL ORDINANCES

CHAPTER 74: ENVIRONMENT

ARTICLE IV. NOISE CONTROL

§ 74-133. Excessive noise.

It shall be unlawful for any person to make, continue or cause to be made or continued any loud or excessive noise which unreasonably interferes with the comfort, response, health and safety of others within the jurisdiction of the city.

Penalties

Depending on the jurisdiction, noise violations may constitute a misdemeanor.

The municipal code of Cincinnati, Ohio is an example of such a statute:

CINCINNATI MUNICIPAL CODE: MISDEMEANORS

§ 910-7. Loud Noises.

No person, firm or corporation shall operate or cause to be operated any whistle, rattle, bell, gong, clapper, hammer, drum, horn, radio, phonograph or other sound-producing or sound-amplifying instrument so as to emit loud and raucous noises or in any other way create noise or sound in such a manner as to disturb the peace and quiet of a neighborhood or as to interfere with the transaction of business or other ordinary pursuits . . . [W]hoever violates this section is guilty of making loud noises, a minor misdemeanor.

Depending on the jurisdiction, the criminal penalties may range from a fine, imprisonment or both.

The City of Jacksonville, Florida has a typical ordinance:

ORDINANCE CODE: CITY OF JACKSONVILLE, FLORIDA

TITLE X. ENVIRONMENTAL AFFAIRS

CHAPTER 368. NOISE CONTROL

PART 1. GENERAL PROVISIONS

PART 4. VIOLATIONS AND PENALTIES

§ 368.401 Violations and criminal penalties.

(a) A person who knowingly and willfully or by culpable negligence commits a violation specified in 368.401(c)(1), (2) (3), (4), and (5) Ordinance Code, may, upon conviction by a court of appropriate jurisdiction thereof, be punished by:

(1) A fine of not more than five hundred dollars; or

(2) Not more than ninety days in jail; or both.

PROPERTY UPKEEP

If you live in a planned development, there are probably strict rules requiring you to maintain your property, e.g., to mow your lawn, fix a broken fence, remove trash, etc. However, if you live in a private home, there are no strict rules on how you take care of your property.

Blighted Property

Most municipalities have ordinances against "blighted property"—i.e., property that becomes so run down it is an eyesore. The Town of Trumbull, Connecticut blight prevention ordinance defines blighted property as:

"Real property, including any building or structure located thereon, which is and continues to be in a state of disrepair or is becoming dilapidated."

Some of the conditions listed as examples of "blighted property" include:

1. Multiple missing, broken or boarded up windows and/or doors;

2. Collapsing or missing walls or roof;

3. Seriously damaged or missing siding;

4. Fire or water damage;

5. Infestation by rodents or other pests;

6. Excessive amounts of garbage or trash on the property;

7. Inoperative or unregistered motor vehicles or inoperative boats parked, kept or stored on the premises unless garaged on the premises;

8. Overgrown brush and/or overgrown grass or weeds of at least one foot in height, excluding ornamental grass as part of a landscaped property;

9. Graffiti; and

10. Any other evidence that reasonably demonstrates that a property would cause an unsafe or unsanitary condition or a nuisance to the general public.

Reporting the Problem

Neighbors become concerned when a home in the neighborhood becomes run down because a blighted property decreases the value of the surrounding properties. If attempts at convincing the property owner to make repairs and clean up the property are ignored, you should make a complaint with the appropriate authorities provided there is an ordinance against blighted property.

In general, there will be an investigation into the complaint and the owner of the blighted property will be issued a warning notice listing the violations and a date by which they must be remedied, and the fines, penalties and costs the owner will face if they fail to comply. If the owner ignores the warning notice, a citation will be issued and the owner will be assessed with the fines, penalties and/or costs outlined in the notice.

For example, the Trumbull, Connecticut ordinance assesses the following penalties on owners of blighted properties:

Section 6. Violations of the provisions of this ordinance shall be punishable by a fine of $100 per day for each day a violation continues to exist. The date the citation was issued shall be the commencement date for said $100 fine.

Unpaid fines and enforcement costs also become a lien on the property, which must be paid before the owner can obtain clear title to the property. In some jurisdictions, blighted property offenses are considered a misdemeanor and the owner may receive jail time for failing to obey the law.

WATER DAMAGE

Water can cause considerable damage to property, including flooded basements, saturated soil, and structural damage. In general, you cannot sue for damage caused by natural water runoff from your neighbor's property, e.g., due to rain or snow. If that is the way the land naturally lies, it is not your neighbor's fault and you will have to find a way to divert the water runoff away from your property.

However, if your neighbor's home improvement project causes a drain pipe to burst, or they landscape their property in a way that causes more water to run onto your property, your neighbor may be liable, if their alteration of the land was unreasonable. For example, if your neighbor installs a pond near your property line, with no drainage plan, and every time it rains, your backyard becomes saturated and unusable, you can sue for damages. You can also ask the court to order your neighbor to remove the pond if he or she cannot repair the drainage problem.

Your neighbor is also liable if he or she is careless, e.g., he forgets to turn off the garden hose, goes away for the weekend, and the water pours down the driveway, into your basement. If you were also away for the weekend, a considerable amount of flooding could occur in that time period.

If you sue and the court agrees that your neighbor's actions were unreasonable and/or careless, and caused the water damage, you are entitled to damages, which may include monetary compensation for the cost of repairs and any related expenses.

You should check with your insurance agent to find out whether you are covered for the water damage caused by your neighbor. If you are covered, your insurance company will likely cover your repairs and then sue your neighbor for reimbursement pursuant to your policy. Most insurance policies give the insurer the right to subrogation. Basically, subrogation is defined as the substitution of the insurer in place of the insured as it relates to a claim against a third party for indemnification of a loss paid by the insurer.

CHAPTER 6:
PREMISES LIABILITY

IN GENERAL

Accidents do happen, however, sometimes an accident occurs because one person did something they shouldn't have done, or failed to do something they should have done. In short, someone's negligence caused the accident. Premises liability is an area of personal injury law that is concerned with injuries sustained on premises that are owned or maintained by another as a result of a dangerous or unsafe condition located on that property.

Thus, if you are on your neighbor's property and injure yourself as a result of a dangerous condition on their property, your neighbor may be liable for your injuries. On the other hand, if your neighbor is injured on your land, you may find yourself legally responsible for his or her injuries.

In order to prevail in a premises liability lawsuit, the owner of the property must have been negligent in some way which caused an unsafe condition on the property, and the injuries must have been "caused" by this unsafe or dangerous condition.

PROTECT YOURSELF – LIABILITY INSURANCE

As a homeowner, it is vital that you obtain liability insurance to cover you for accidents that occur on your property. You may be held liable and have to pay injury claims out of your own pocket if you do not carry an insurance liability policy.

For example, if there has been a recent snowfall, you are responsible for clearing the snow and ice off of your sidewalk within a reasonable amount of time following the precipitation so that pedestrians are able to walk on the sidewalk without the risk of falling. If your neighbor—or any pedestrian—walks in front of your home, falls on the snow and sustain injuries and you do not have liability insurance, you may be liable for that person's medical bills and related costs, lost wages, and pain and suffering.

If, despite the preventive measures taken, an accident still occurs and someone is injured on your property, you should promptly notify your insurance carrier. In fact, most insurance policies have a requirement that the insured notify the insurance company of any potential claim within a certain period of time after an incident occurs. Do not discuss the incident directly with the injured party or their representative. Refer all correspondence and phone calls to your insurance carrier.

It is also prudent to document the incident. For example, take photographs of the area immediately following the accident. Write down any statements made by the injured party. Record the facts so that you can refresh your memory when your insurance claims representative and/or attorney ask you for a statement.

If you have any information that would lead you to believe the injured person was responsible for his or her own injuries—e.g., because they were careless or intoxicated—you should obtain the names, addresses and telephone numbers of any witnesses who saw the incident and will support your contentions.

MAKE IMMEDIATE REPAIRS

You should also immediately remedy the condition that caused the accident in the first place, if in fact there was such a condition. The fact that someone was injured on your property by whatever condition existed places you on notice. If another person were injured as a result of the same condition, it would be extremely difficult to defend that claim.

In general, the fact that you take steps to make repairs on an unsafe condition on your property following an accident generally cannot be used as evidence of liability in a lawsuit. There is a public safety concern that property owners maintain their premises in a safe condition. If a property owner risked being found liable in a lawsuit because they made repairs to their property following an accident, they would be less likely to make the repairs, thus putting the public at risk.

TRESPASS

Under the common law, a property owner is not liable to a trespasser for injuries caused by the owner's failure to exercise reasonable care to make the land safe. However, an owner who knows, or should know, that there are trespassers who constantly intrude on the property is liable for bodily harm caused them by an unsafe condition on the property if:

1. The condition is one the owner created or maintained;

2. The condition is likely to cause death or serious bodily harm;

3. The condition is of such a nature that the owner has reason to believe that trespassers will not discover it; and

4. The owner has failed to exercise reasonable care to warn trespassers of the condition and risk involved.

For example, if you are aware that your neighbor routinely enters your property to trim the branches on a boundary tree, and you recently dug a large hole in that same area for a tree you intend to plant, you have a duty to place some type of barricade or sign around the hole to alert your neighbor of the dangerous condition. If you leave the hole uncovered, or simply cover the hole with a tarp, and your neighbor falls in the hole and breaks his or her leg, you may be held liable for your neighbor's injuries.

ATTRACTIVE NUISANCE

An attractive nuisance is a condition existing on your property that is potentially harmful, and so inviting or interesting to a child, that it would lure the child onto the property to play with it or explore the area. A common example of an attractive nuisance is an unenclosed swimming pool that would be very inviting to your neighbor's 4-year old son, who because of his age and inexperience would be unaware of the extent of the danger.

Property owners have a special legal responsibility to try to prevent injuries to children who may wander onto the property even though the child is technically a "trespasser" on the premises. According to the Restatement of Torts, a property owner or possessor is liable for an injury to trespassing children if:

1. The place where the condition is maintained is one where the owner knows or should know that young children are likely to trespass;

2. The condition is one of which the possessor knows, or should know, and which he realized or should realize as involving unreasonable risk of death or serious bodily harm to such children;

3. The children, because of their youth, do not discover the condition or realize the risk involved in coming within the area made dangerous by it; and

4. The utility to the possessor of maintaining the condition is slight as compared to the risk to young children who trespass thereon.

In addition, the age of the child would be taken into consideration in determining the extent to which they should have realized the danger.

It is important to regularly inspect your property to see whether there are any potentially dangerous conditions that might attract children. If so, you should take immediate action to rectify the unsafe condition. In addition, you should be aware of any local building code requirements that govern.

For example, because of the high incidence of drowning deaths among young children, most jurisdictions have zoning regulations concerning swimming pools. Commonly, a swimming pool is required to be enclosed in a fence on all four sides. The fence must be a certain height—e.g. 4 feet—and cannot have openings which would allow a young child to climb through or over the fence.

In addition, the enclosure must generally have a self-closing, self-latching gate with the placement of the latch at a certain height so that a small child cannot open it. If you do not comply with these regulations, and a child is injured as a result, you may be held strictly liable for those injuries. A sample provision is as follows:

WEBSTER TOWN CODE – TOWN OF WEBSTER, NEW YORK

CHAPTER 196: SWIMMING POOLS

§ 196-5. Fences.

A. All swimming pools shall be surrounded and totally enclosed by a substantial fence or wall four (4) feet in height to guard against accidental or unauthorized entry. Such fence shall be equipped with a self-closing and self-latching gate capable of being locked with its latch located only on the inside of the gate, except where such swimming pool is suitably protected by a wall or walls of an accessory or main structure on the premises. Any door in the wall or entrances through an accessory or main structure shall also be self-closing and self-latching. Said fence shall not be of a nature so as to be dangerous in and of itself and shall have no opening larger than two (2) inches in width and shall be placed a minimum of four (4) feet from the walls of the swimming pool.

CHAPTER 7:
ANIMALS

IN GENERAL

Most jurisdictions have laws that regulate animal ownership and place certain restrictions on animal owners. There are leash laws that prevent dogs from running at large, and regulations on the number of pets an individual may own. A pet owner cannot let their dog bark all night, or allow their cat to roam onto another's property and rummage through the garbage cans, causing a mess.

If you are having a problem with your neighbor's pet, you should get a copy of the law concerning animal ownership in your town to find out if there is an ordinance that governs the situation. When trying to resolve a pet problem with your neighbor, it is always good to know you have the law on your side. Show your neighbor the section of law that is being violated. In most cases, the pet owner is unaware of the law and, once notified, will address the problem.

If you are unable to amicably resolve the problem with your neighbor, you will have to ask your local animal control department to enforce the law. It is particularly helpful if you can point to the specific section of law that has been violated. Typical animal ordinances are set forth below.

LICENSING REQUIREMENTS

Most laws require both cats and dogs to be licensed and that the animals wear their license tags at all times. Licensing is an important element in animal control and the protection of the public health. Information about licensed dogs assists in the medical follow-up of persons potentially exposed to infected dogs. In order to obtain a license, you must generally provide proof that your pet has been vaccinated against rabies. Licensing also helps to reunite lost dogs with their owners. If the owner does not obtain a license for their pet as required by law, he or she may be fined.

A typical animal licensing law under the New York City Health Code is as follows:

Title 24 § 161.04 Dog Licenses

(b) Every person who owns, possesses or controls a dog shall not permit it to be in any public place, or in any open or unfenced area abutting on a public place, unless the dog has a collar about its neck with a currently valid metal tag attached thereto bearing the number of the license obtained for such dog. (24 RCNY Health Code Reg. § 161.04)

LEASH LAWS

Most jurisdictions require that dog owners have their dog on a leash when walking the dog in public or in an open area. It is a violation for any person to permit their dog to be "at large." A typical animal leash law under the New York City Health Code is as follows:

Title 24 § 161.05 Dog to be restrained

A person who owns, possesses or controls a dog shall not permit it to be in any public place or in any open or unfenced area abutting on a public place unless the dog is effectively restrained by a leash or chain not more than six feet long. (24 RCNY Health Code Reg. § 161.05)

The term "at large" refers to an animal that is not under the physical control of a person by means of a leash, cord or chain, or not in the physical presence of its owner or other person responsible for the animal. "At large" also refers to a dog that is not confined to the property of its owner by means of a fence. It is also against the law to tie, chain or tether a dog to public property or property belonging to another person.

Therefore, as friendly as your neighbor's golden retriever may be, it is against the law for the animal to run loose and bury its bones in your backyard. If a dog is found "at large" by an animal control officer, and the dog does not have a license or other means of identification, it is generally transported to an animal shelter. If the dog is licensed, the animal control officer may return the dog to its residence and issue a citation to the pet's owner.

In general, cats are considered free roaming animals, and are not required to be confined on a leash. However, if a cat poses a nuisance, a property owner may have the right to catch the cat and have it taken to the animal shelter.

CANINE WASTE LAWS

It is generally against the law for any person to allow their pet to defecate on public property and on private property not belonging to the animal's owner unless the dog owner makes every effort to immediately clean up and dispose of the dog's droppings in a sanitary manner. Violators may face penalties for failure to do so. Owners of assistance dogs are usually exempt from these laws.

NUISANCE PETS AND BARKING DOGS

If you live next door to a dog that barks all night, or a cat that regularly rummages through the trash cans on your property, you really can't blame the animals for doing what animals do. You can, however, go to the pet's owner to try and get some relief. It may be that your neighbor is unaware that their pet is causing such a disturbance. If you are on good terms with your neighbor, you can usually work out some type of agreement, e.g., the dog will not be left outside during the overnight hours, or the cat will be restricted to a fenced in area of the yard.

You can also try mediation, if your neighbor is willing to join you, in order to work out some mutually satisfactory solution with the assistance of an impartial mediator. Mediators are trained to help individuals focus on the disputed issues and make constructive suggestions on how to solve the problem without letting the discussion escalate into argument.

Mediation is discussed more fully in Chapter 9 of this almanac.

Nevertheless, if your neighbor takes a defensive position and is unwilling to fix the problem, there are public nuisance and noise restriction laws in most jurisdictions. You can contact animal control authorities or the local police and ask them to enforce these laws. A typical "barking dog" ordinance reads as follows:

CODE OF ORDINANCES: CITY OF ATLANTA, GEORGIA

PART II CODE OF ORDINANCES—GENERAL ORDINANCES

CHAPTER 74: ENVIRONMENT

ARTICLE IV. NOISE CONTROL

(5) Animals. The owning, possessing or harboring of any animal which frequently or continuously howls, barks, meows, squawks or makes other sounds which create excessive noise across a residential or commercial real property line or within a noise-sensitive area. For the purpose of this article, barking dogs shall include a dog that barks, bays, cries, howls or makes any

other noise continuously for a period of ten minutes, or barks intermittently for one-half hour or more to the disturbance at any time of day or night regardless of whether the dog is physically situated in or upon private property.

If all else fails, you may have to bring a nuisance lawsuit in small claims court, however, suing your neighbor can be time consuming, costly and an unpleasant experience, and should only be used as your last resort. If you prove your case in court, the judge may fine the pet owner, and/or may issue an order setting forth certain conditions concerning the offending dog, e.g., mandatory obedience training. If the animal destroyed property belonging to you, you may be able to recover monetary damages.

The procedure of filing a small claims court case is discussed in Chapter 10 of this almanac.

DOG BITE LIABILITY

Every year, more than 4.7 million people are bitten by dogs, many of whom require medical intervention for their injuries. If a dog bites someone, the owner is usually held liable provided:

1. The owner knew the dog had a tendency to bite;

2. There is a state statute that makes the owner liable regardless of whether or not the owner knew the dog had a tendency to bite (a "strict liability" statute); or

3. The owner was unreasonably careless.

The owner is liable not only for dog bites, but for any other injuries that the dog may cause.

Defenses

Under certain circumstances, a dog owner may not be held liable. For example, liability may be avoided if:

1. The owner can prove that the injured person provoked the injury, e.g., the victim hit or teased the dog, or accidentally hurt the dog;

2. The victim voluntarily and knowingly risked being injured by the dog, e.g. by ignoring warning signs;

3. The victim was trespassing or breaking the law; or

4. The victim was being unreasonably careless around the dog, which contributed to the victim's injury.

Nevertheless, if you are being attacked by a dog, or witness a dog attack, under most state laws, you are permitted to take whatever action is necessary to stop the attack, including killing the dog.

The "One-Bite" Rule

A number of jurisdictions have what is known as the "one bite rule." Basically, this rule means that the owner is only liable for injuries caused by their dog if he or she knew that the dog was likely to bite someone. Once a dog bites someone, or tries to bite someone, the owner is automatically placed on notice that the dog is a biter, and the owner will be liable for any future injuries caused by the dog.

The following jurisdictions follow the "one bite" rule: Alaska, Arkansas, Colorado, Delaware, Georgia, Idaho, Kansas, Maryland, Mississippi, Missouri, Nevada, New Mexico, New York, North Carolina, North Dakota, Oregon, South Dakota, Tennessee, Texas, Vermont, Virginia, and Wyoming.

Damages

The dog's owner will generally be responsible for the costs the bite victim incurs as a result of being bitten, such as medical bills, lost wages, and the victim's pain and suffering. Homeowner's insurance usually covers a dog bite claim, however, as more fully discussed below, many insurance companies are refusing to insure homeowners who harbor certain breeds of dogs that are considered inherently dangerous.

As more fully discussed below, if a complaint is brought against the dog to determine whether it should be declared a "dangerous dog," a hearing will determine whether the owner must destroy the dog or whether there will be strict requirements imposed on the owner if he or she wishes to keep the dog.

Taking Action Following a Dog Attack

If you are bitten or otherwise attacked by your neighbor's dog, you must immediately alert animal control so that they can seize the dog and have it confined and quarantined for a period of time to make sure it doesn't have rabies. However, if the owner can provide proof that the animal has been vaccinated, confinement is generally not necessary.

If you arc seriously injured, you should seek immediate medical attention and keep copies of all hospital and medical reports. You should also keep all of the medical bills for which you will be seeking reimbursement from the dog's owner.

You should also check with the local animal control office to find out if the dog that bit you ever bit anyone else, or if the dog has been declared a "dangerous dog," as more fully discussed below. If so, this will make your case much stronger if you have to take the dog owner to court to recover damages.

DANGEROUS DOGS

The majority of dogs are not dangerous, and if they are involved in a biting incident, it is usually because they were being provoked or they are being protective. Nevertheless, as discussed above, once a dog does bite someone, even if it is a one-time occurrence, there are laws in place in many jurisdictions that intervene to identify whether the dog is a threat to public safety. Some of these laws automatically classify certain dogs as dangerous despite whether they have exhibited aggressive behavior, simply because of their breed, e.g., pit bulls.

This legislative effort in the area of dog regulation is due to increasing reports all across the United States that there are certain exceptionally dangerous and unpredictable dogs of various breeds that, once provoked, become uncontrollable lethal weapons, posing significant dangers to unsuspecting and innocent people. Statistics demonstrate that people die as a result of dog attacks, at the rate of one or more a month, and countless others have been hurt and maimed, with children and elderly persons being the most frequent targets.

In order to protect the health and safety of their citizens, many local jurisdictions have enacted "dangerous dog" laws, intended to identify vicious dogs and prevent injuries. A growing number of states have also enacted dangerous dog laws, including: California, Colorado, Delaware, District of Columbia, Florida, Georgia, Hawaii, Illinois, Kentucky, Louisiana, Maine, Maryland, Massachusetts, Michigan, Minnesota, Nebraska, Nevada, New Hampshire, New Jersey, New York, North Carolina, Ohio, Oklahoma, Pennsylvania, Rhode Island, South Carolina, South Dakota, Texas, Vermont, Virginia, Washington, and West Virginia.

In general, the process of having a dog designated as a dangerous animal begins with a formal complaint about the dog by any person, including an animal control officer or person who has been injured by the dog. A hearing is conducted before a judge or other designated official, and evidence may be presented by all interested persons as to the dog's propensity for violence.

Usually, if the dog has already caused severe injury to someone, the dog may be impounded, at the owner's expense, pending the hearing and determination of the complaint. A determination is made, based on the evidence, whether or not the dog falls under the category of a dangerous animal, according to the applicable law.

The law generally excuses the dog if the person who was injured was intentionally trespassing on the dog owner's property, attempting to commit a crime, or was seriously provoking the dog.

If a dog receives an official designation as a dangerous dog, there are special restrictions placed on their owners to prevent the dog from causing injuries, ranging from confinement to destruction of the dog, if it cannot be controlled. If your neighbor violates the court-ordered restrictions, many laws provide that that the dog can be seized and impounded, and the owner may be fined and/or imprisoned.

Further, if it is found that the pet owner deliberately made a dog vicious for the purpose of fighting or causing injury to others, the owner may face more severe fines and/or imprisonment. If a dog that has been trained to be vicious mauls or kills someone, the owner may be charged with a crime, such as manslaughter or murder.

BREED-SPECIFIC RESTRICTIONS

Dog experts disagree that certain breeds of dogs have inherent vicious tendencies, however, injury reports and lawsuits appear to indicate that certain breeds of dog are responsible for the majority of serious injuries. For this reason, many jurisdictions have passed laws prohibiting the possession of certain breeds, such as pit bulls, that are deemed dangerous. Thus, if your neighbor's dog is particularly menacing, you should check your local laws to find out whether the dog is covered under this restriction. If so, report the violation to your local animal control department.

Some jurisdictions do not prohibit these "dangerous" breeds entirely, but do impose strict requirements on the dog owners similar to those imposed on other dogs that are declared dangerous following a hearing, as discussed above.

EXOTIC AND ILLEGAL PETS

Most people keep dogs and cats as family pets. Some prefer smaller animals, such as birds, fish, hamsters, and gerbils. However, every once in a while you hear a story about someone who desires a much more exotic—and potentially dangerous—animal, e.g., a boa constrictor, an alligator, or even a tiger. Most people would not be comfortable knowing that such an animal lived next door.

If you discover that your next-door neighbor is raising a bathtub full of piranha, or worse, it is likely that it is against the law. Not all animals can be kept legally as pets, and others require special permits. Some animals pose too much of a risk to the public to allow people to keep them as pets, therefore, the law either bans them as pets or places restrictions on owning such pets, including special licensing requirements. An example of such a law is as follows:

MUNICIPAL CODE OF THE CITY OF DES MOINES IOWA

CHAPTER 18. ANIMALS

ARTICLE VI. ILLEGAL AND DANGEROUS ANIMALS

Sec. 18-197. Keeping illegal animals prohibited.

No person shall keep, shelter, or harbor any illegal animal as a pet nor act as a temporary custodian for such animal nor keep, shelter, or harbor such animal for any other purpose or in any other capacity within the city, except as provided in section 18-198 of this article.

You can find out whether your neighbor's "pet" is legal by calling the local government agency responsible for licensing animals. They should be able to give you information on the legal status of the animal, or they will direct you to the appropriate government agency. The ASPCA and local animal rescue organizations, animal shelters, humane societies, veterinarians and pet shops may also be helpful. In addition, you may be able to find information about the particular species on the Internet.

If you find out that your neighbor is harbouring an illegal pet, you should contact your local animal control authorities. They will investigate and remove any illegal animal. For example, the Iowa statute provides as follows:

MUNICIPAL CODE OF THE CITY OF DES MOINES IOWA

CHAPTER 18. ANIMALS

ARTICLE VI. ILLEGAL AND DANGEROUS ANIMALS

Sec. 18-199. Seizure, impoundment and disposition of illegal animals.

(b) Upon the complaint of an individual that a person is keeping, sheltering, or harboring an illegal animal on premises in the city, the chief humane officer shall cause the matter to be investigated. If, after investigation, the facts indicate that the person named in the complaint is keeping, sheltering or harboring an illegal animal in the city, the chief humane officer shall immediately seize any such animal. An animal so seized shall be impounded for a period of seven days. If at the end of the impoundment period the individual or entity keeping, sheltering or harboring such illegal animal has not petitioned the county district court seeking return of such illegal animal, the chief humane officer shall cause the animal to be disposed of by sale, shall permanently place such animal with an organization or group allowed under section 18-198 of this article to possess illegal animals, or shall destroy such animal in a humane manner.

CHAPTER 8:
ILLEGAL ACTIVITIES

IN GENERAL

Many of the activities discussed in this almanac involve day-to-day problems with a neighbor that may be inconvenient, may cause a nuisance, may even result in property damage. However, as discussed below, when certain illegal activities invade the neighborhood, they pose a much more serious—as well as potentially dangerous—problem, and require immediate action.

DRUG DEALERS

You may notice strangers in the neighborhood, entering and exiting a certain house on the block, or apartment in the building, at all hours of the day, but particularly at night. The people living in the house may be renters who don't appear to work outside the home, and pay the landlord in cash. The windows may be blacked out or covered, and you may smell an unusual odor coming from the house. There may be security cameras or guard dogs protecting the house.

These are all markers of drug dealing, and may even indicate that a methamphetamine lab or crack house now exists in the midst of your formerly safe, quiet neighborhood. Drug dealing brings other negative elements into the neighborhood, criminal activity soars, and thus begins the downfall of the neighborhood. For this reason, any indication of suspicious behavior should be investigated and dealt with swiftly. You should organize a group of law-abiding residents, and meet with the local law enforcement authorities to discuss the problem. If the house is rented, notify the owner that the house is being used to traffic drugs, and demand that the owner immediately begin eviction proceedings against the tenants.

If the owner ignores the problem, your group should consider hiring a lawyer and bringing a public nuisance action against the owner, as well as the tenants. In some cases, state and federal laws allow the government to seize property that is being used for illegal financial gain. The threat of losing the property may motivate the owner to evict the tenants.

Until the problem is resolved, continue to gather evidence. For example, keep log books detailing the activities, and write down the license plate numbers of cars that frequent the house. This evidence can help bolster a case in court, and may spur local law enforcement into taking action.

ILLEGAL APARTMENTS

If you notice a larger than usual number of people living in an apartment or home in your neighborhood, particularly if those people appear to be unrelated, you may have stumbled upon a growing problem—illegal apartments. Many landlords unlawfully rent out all of the rooms in a house or apartment, often to illegal immigrants. Sometimes, it is the tenants themselves who rent out the other rooms in the house or apartment. Living conditions are often deplorable in these illegal multi-unit dwellings, and illegal immigrants are too afraid to report their living conditions to the authorities for fear of deportation.

These "rooming houses" cause many problems in the neighborhood. They are overcrowded and pose fire and safety hazards. The properties often become blighted because the tenants cannot afford the upkeep, and the landlords just pocket the money without regard to health, safety or living conditions. There is a drain on services, and schools become overcrowded and underfunded, as the landlord only pays property and school taxes based on a single family dwelling, and the tenants pay no taxes whatsoever. The numerous cars owned by the tenants take up all of the parking spaces on a block zoned for one-family homes.

Illegal apartments violate town ordinances. Following is a typical zoning ordinance that prohibits landlords from renting illegal apartments, and subjects the landlord to penalties:

BOROUGH OF WEST PATERSON—ILLEGAL DWELLING ORDINANCE

ORDINANCE NO. 06-05

§ 2. Illegal apartment or dwelling unit:

B. No person shall rent, or allow to be occupied, an "illegal" apartment or dwelling unit, or permit same to be occupied by any tenant or other person, in:

(1) a building which such person owns or otherwise controls;

(2) a dwelling unit which such person rents or otherwise controls.

§ 6. Violations:

A. [A]ny person who violates this Chapter shall be subject to the following fines:

(1) for the first offense, a mandatory fine of $1,500.00 shall be imposed;

(2) for the second offense, a mandatory fine of $5,000.00 shall be imposed;

(3) for the third offense and all subsequent offenses, a mandatory fine of $8,000.00 shall be imposed or imprisonment for a term not to exceed ninety (90) days, or both.

If you suspect that a house in your neighborhood is being used as an illegal rooming house, you should contact the zoning violation bureau, as well as your local law enforcement authorities. Some communities have established hotlines for residents to leave anonymous tips regarding illegal apartments.

SEX OFFENDERS

One of the most disturbing problems facing families today is the presence of a sex offender or pedophile in the neighborhood. This concern is well-founded. As of July 1, 2005, there were 563,806 registered sex offenders in the United States. Studies show that sex offenders pose a high risk of repeat behavior following their conviction or release from prison. Thus, it was recognized that there was a need for legislation to protect the public, especially children, from these sexual predators.

The Jacob Wetterling Crimes Against Children and Sexually Violent Offender Act of 1994

Following the 1989 abduction and murder of 11-year old Jacob Wetterling in Minnesota by a recently released sex offender, Congress passed the *Jacob Wetterling Crimes Against Children and Sexually Violent Offender Act* in 1994. Under the Act, all states are required to implement a sex-offender registration program. Individuals convicted of sexually related crimes are required to register as sex offenders with the state after conviction, or if they serve time in prison, upon their release.

Sex offenders must also notify the state's registry when they relocate. If a registrant changes his or her address, they are required to update their registration information within a specified number of days. The states track the dates of the sex offender's required updates and, if a registered sex offender fails to update their information by the deadline, they are in violation of the law.

Megan's Law - Community Notification

In 1994, 7-year old Megan Kanka accepted an invitation from a neighbor in Hamilton Township, New Jersey, to see his new puppy. Unknown to the community, the neighbor was a twice-convicted pedophile. He raped Megan, murdered her, and dumped her body in a nearby park.

Following this tragedy, there was outrage over Megan's tragic and unnecessary murder. Megan's parents said that they would never have allowed her to travel the neighborhood freely if they had known that a convicted sex offender was living across the street. The public demanded to know whether child molesters were also living in their neighborhood. The Kanka family joined in the fight for a community notification law that would warn the public about sex offenders living in their area.

Realizing that the sex offender registration requirement under the *Jacob Wetterling Act* did not adequately protect the public, particularly the children who are most vulnerable to child sexual predators, legislators responded by passing a federal law mandating state community notification programs. On May 17, 1996, *Megan's Law* was enacted as an amendment to the *Jacob Wetterling Act*.

Under *Megan's Law*, all states are required to implement a community notification program and maintain sex offender websites where sex offender information is posted and made accessible to the public. Since the passage of the federal legislation, all states have passed some form of *Megan's Law*.

Different states have different procedures for making the required disclosures. In general, the statutes set forth three levels of sex offenders: Level 1 (low risk), Level 2 (moderate risk), and Level 3 (high risk). Local law enforcement generally decides whether to notify the public about Level 2 and 3 offenders, however, information about Level 1 offenders is not usually made public.

Search the Registry

You do not have to wait for a postcard in the mail notifying you that your neighbor is a registered sex offender. This is information you should have immediately. You cannot be too careful when it comes to the safety of your children.

You can find out whether a sexual predator is living in your neighborhood on the Internet. On most websites, you need only enter your address and a list of registered sex offenders in your area will be retrieved. The website generally contains a photograph of the offender, as well as background information about the offender, and details on the offense committed.

Although you may not be able to force the offender out of the neighborhood, you can take the proper precautions to protect your loved ones, and the other residents of your neighborhood.

A directory of state sex offender registration websites is set forth at Appendix 11.

CHAPTER 9:
MEDIATION

WHAT IS MEDIATION?

Mediation is a completely voluntary type of alternative dispute resolution. It is more economical and less time-consuming than going to court. As mediation can be scheduled at an early stage in the dispute, a settlement can be reached much more quickly than in litigation.

If you and your neighbor have an otherwise amicable relationship, but have been unable to resolve your controversy because you both believe you are right, it may be helpful to involve a third party who can be objective. You and your neighbor can agree to submit your dispute to mediation and attempt to salvage your relationship through negotiation, rather than go to court as adversaries and further alienate one another.

A sample agreement to mediate a dispute is set forth at Appendix 12.

During mediation, a neutral third person—known as a mediator—helps the parties to a dispute discuss their problem and work out their own mutually acceptable solution. It is a private and confidential procedure thus information disclosed at a mediation may not be divulged as evidence in any other proceeding.

A mediator is carefully chosen for his or her knowledge and experience. As a neutral third party, the mediator is able to view the dispute objectively, and can therefore assist the parties in exploring alternatives that they might not have considered on their own. However, the mediator cannot force the parties to change their positions, and does not issue a binding decision.

It is the mediator's role to assist the opposing parties in resolving their own dispute. The parties remain responsible for negotiating a settlement of their dispute, which may then be formalized in a written agreement. Thus, for mediation to be successful, the parties who agree to mediate their dispute must do so with a cooperative spirit and a good faith willingness to mediate.

THE AMERICAN ARBITRATION ASSOCIATION

The American Arbitration Association (AAA) is a non-profit organization that was formed to help parties resolve a wide range of disputes through mediation and other forms of dispute resolution. Mediators are available to assist parties in resolving their disputes. If the parties want to use mediation through the AAA, they may do so under the AAA's Commercial Mediation Rules. Additional information may be obtained by visiting the AAA website at www.adr.org.

A directory of AAA Regional Offices is set forth at Appendix 13.

CHOOSING A MEDIATOR

Choosing the right mediator for your particular situation is crucial to achieving a successful result. An interview with the prospective mediator should be conducted to ascertain the mediator's background, methods and demeanor. A list of questions should be prepared in advance covering all pertinent areas of concern.

Because the mediator is a neutral party, he or she does not advocate for either side. The mediator presents the issues in a structured and informative manner, encouraging communication and cooperation, in an effort to guide the participants to a successful resolution of their controversy.

Professional mediators often have backgrounds and hold degrees in the areas of psychology and sociology. Such experience is particularly useful when dealing with the intense display of human emotions that commonly emerge in the course of a dispute. Professional mediators may also have expertise in other related fields, however, issues may arise that are sufficiently complex to warrant hiring other professionals, e.g., a certified arborist if the case involves tree damage.

The American Arbitration Association Model Standards for Mediators is set forth at Appendix 14.

THE MEDIATION PROCEDURE

After choosing a mediator, you and your neighbor will meet with the mediator to discuss the issues of the dispute. Each side is given the opportunity to express their position. The mediator explains the mediation procedure and answers any questions you and your neighbor may have.

Following your initial meeting together, the mediator will meet with you and your neighbor individually so that each of you can express your positions clearly and openly. During the individual sessions, the mediator presents and discusses each party's concerns with the other party, in an effort to reach some common ground.

After meeting with each party individually, the mediator may schedule another session with everyone present to determine whether there has been any progress. The process of meeting individually and jointly continues until a settlement is obtained—if possible—in which case the mediator will assist the parties in formalizing their written agreement.

Most mediation cases are settled in a few hours. Others may require additional time, depending on the complexity of the issues. Although mediation itself is not binding, a signed settlement agreement is as enforceable as any other contractual agreement. A properly executed agreement may be used in litigation should one of the parties breach the terms of the agreement.

SETTLEMENT

The controversy between you and your neighbor may be settled at any stage of the mediation. Once an agreement has been reached, a final written document encompassing all of the negotiated points should be drafted and signed by the parties. Depending on the nature of the dispute, a settlement agreement may also include a release of claims. By signing a release, a party gives up all right to pursue the claims stated in the release. This is both the motivation and consideration for entering into the settlement agreement.

A sample settlement agreement and release of claims is set forth at Appendix 15.

CHAPTER 10:
THE LAST RESORT: SMALL CLAIMS COURT

IN GENERAL

If you tried unsuccessfully to amicably resolve the problem you have with your neighbor, he or she wouldn't agree to mediation, and law enforcement refused to take action, your only alternative may be to sue your neighbor in small claims court. A small claims court is a low-level court that provides individuals with the ability to bring an informal legal action against another party without having to hire an attorney. A small claims action is relatively inexpensive and less time-consuming than bringing a lawsuit in a higher court.

Most small claims courts have clerks who are available to provide the necessary forms, and assist the parties with general information on starting and defending a small claims action. However, these clerks are not permitted to provide legal advice to the litigants. Depending on the jurisdiction, the parties may be permitted to hire a lawyer to represent them in small claims court, however, it is not necessary and the cost of doing so is generally prohibitive considering the jurisdictional limit on monetary damages.

MONETARY LIMIT

There is a limit on the amount of money you can sue for in small claims court, depending on the jurisdiction. If your claim exceeds the jurisdictional limit, and you decide to proceed in small claims court, any amount over the jurisdictional limit is deemed waived. You are not permitted to bring two separate actions against the defendant for the same claim in order to recover the total amount sought—a prohibited practice known as "claim-splitting."

For example, if you are seeking $3,000 in damages from your neighbor for damaging some expensive shrubbery on your property, and the jurisdictional limit is $2,000, you cannot bring two separate actions against your neighbor based upon the same set of facts, in order to recover the total amount. If you decide to proceed with the small claims action, you will have to waive the additional $1,000 in damages.

A table setting forth the monetary limits for cases filed in each state small claim court is set forth at Appendix 16.

JURISDICTION

In order to start a small claims action, you must file your claim in the small claims court that has jurisdiction over the claim. You can check with the clerk of the court to determine the proper venue for the action. Generally, proper venue would be the court located in the jurisdiction where you and your neighbor live. If you file the action in an improper venue, the judge will dismiss the action unless the defendant agrees to allow the court to hear the case. If the case is dismissed, it must be refiled in the proper venue in order to proceed.

Most small-claims courts can award money only. If you want your neighbor to remove a fence or tree, or you want an injunction to get your neighbor to stop making noise or cease certain activities that constitute a nuisance, you will generally have to file your lawsuit in a higher court, and you will need to hire an attorney because the procedure is more complex.

Nevertheless, if you are suing for monetary compensation related to a nuisance or noise problem, you can generally sue over and over as long as the problem continues. Thus, if your neighbor refuses to cooperate, you can keep bringing small claims actions and recover monetary awards until your neighbor finally gives in and corrects the problem.

A directory of state small claims court information websites is set forth at Appendix 17.

LIABILITY

Before beginning the small claims action, it is wise to consider the likelihood that you will prevail in the lawsuit. Your neighbor must be liable—i.e., legally responsible—in order for you to recover and obtain a judgment. Your neighbor's actions may be extremely annoying to you, but not necessarily illegal or tortious. As set forth in this almanac, you should research the law as it applies to your claim prior to filing the case to make sure you are not wasting your time. The judge is obligated to follow and apply the law to the facts of the case, even if the outcome appears unjust.

PREPARING THE SMALL CLAIMS COMPLAINT

The clerk of the court will provide you with the legal forms necessary to begin the small claims action. You will need to prepare a statement of your claim, which includes the basic facts and the amount of damages you are seeking. The statement setting forth your claim is generally referred to as a complaint, and you are known as the "plaintiff." Your neighbor—the neighbor you are suing—is called the "defendant."

Different states use different types of forms for initiating a small claims action, therefore, the reader is advised to check with the clerk of the court for specific requirements in completing the complaint.

A Notice, Claim and Summons to Appear for Trial (CO) is set forth at Appendix 18; a Statement of Claim (ME) is set forth at Appendix 19; and a Small Claims Writ and Notice of Suit (CT) is set forth at Appendix 20, as examples of the various types of state forms used for initiating a small claims action.

The complaint forms must be filed with the clerk of the court, at which time you will have to pay a filing fee. The court will set a date and time for a hearing which both you and your neighbor are required to attend. In most jurisdictions, the hearing is basically a pre-trial appearance during which the Court will discuss how to proceed with the trial, if the case cannot be resolved at the hearing.

SERVING THE COMPLAINT

Once the complaint has been filed, it must be served on your neighbor so that he or she has notice of the claim and the hearing date. This is known as "service of process." "Personal service" is usually the method by which the complaint must be served. Personal service may be made by any person over the age of 18 who is not a party to the action. This person may be a friend or relative. In some jurisdictions, the sheriff may serve the legal papers on your neighbor. In addition, there are professional process servers who will serve legal papers for a fee. Personal service requires that the complaint be given to the individually named defendant, in person, or to a person who is authorized to receive service on their behalf.

A trial cannot proceed unless there is proof that your neighbor has been served and is aware of the pending action. You are generally required to file proof of service with the Court, usually in the form of a sworn and notarized affidavit by the person who served the complaint.

The reader is advised to check with the clerk of the court in their own jurisdiction to determine the type of service that is required and whether any alternative methods of service will suffice.

DISCONTINUING THE ACTION

Sometimes being served with a lawsuit is enough to get your neighbor to negotiate. If you and your neighbor are able to resolve the problem, you can discontinue the small claims action. To do so, you must advise the court of your intentions. If you discontinue the action "without prejudice," this means that you are maintaining the right to sue your neighbor in the future on the same claim—e.g., if your neighbor reneges on the agreement—provided the statute of limitations does not expire in the interim.

> EXAMPLE: You serve your neighbor with a lawsuit claiming he or she did not pay their share of maintenance expenses for a boundary fence. Your neighbor contacts you, apologizes, and agrees to reimburse you as soon as he or she receives his income tax refund. You agree to discontinue the action "without prejudice." Your neighbor reneges on the promise. You can go back to small claims court and bring the same action you discontinued provided the statute of limitations has not yet expired. On the other hand, if you discontinue the action "with prejudice," this means that you are giving up your right to sue your neighbor in the future on the same claim.

> EXAMPLE: You serve your neighbor with a lawsuit claiming your neighbor damaged some bushes located on your property. Your neighbor contacts you, apologizes, and agrees to reimburse you for the cost of replacing the bushes. You agree to discontinue the action "with prejudice." Your neighbor reneges on the promise. You cannot go back to small claims court and bring an action for the damage to your bushes. However, if your neighbor subsequently damages a tree located on your property, you can bring a new claim for the loss of that tree.

Nevertheless, you can still sue your neighbor on future claims, or if he or she continues the same activities, such as continuing to play loud music at all hours of the night, interfering with the quiet enjoyment of your property.

THE STATUTE OF LIMITATIONS

A statute of limitations refers to any law which fixes the time within which an individual must take judicial action to enforce his or her rights. If a claim isn't filed within the time limit set by the particular statute, the claim will be dismissed. The reason there is a statute of limitations is to avoid the filing of old cases which may not be as reliable due to lack of memory, disappearance or death of witnesses, etc. Thus, you are advised to file your claim as soon as possible.

THE PRELIMINARY HEARING

If both you and your neighbor appear at the preliminary hearing, and the case is settled at that time, there are no further proceedings, and you and your neighbor will sign a settlement agreement. If you cannot reach an agreement, a trial date will be set.

If your neighbor does not appear, the Court may order a default judgment if it is satisfied that your neighbor was properly served and thus had notice of the action. In that case, the Court may order an inquest, as discussed below, and award damages based upon your evidence.

PREPARING FOR TRIAL

The time it takes for your case to go to trial varies according to the jurisdiction and the court's docket. Before proceeding to trial, you must gather all of the evidence you need in order to prove your claim. Evidence may be in the form of witness testimony, writings—e.g., warning letters you sent to your neighbor, estimates, photographs, police reports, incident reports, and anything else you may have that will prove your side of the story.

Insofar as small claims court is designed to be informal, the judge may consider evidence that may not be admissible in a higher court. Therefore, if you think a particular piece of evidence might help your case, bring it to court whether or not you believe it is admissible.

It is always best to present the original document in court, if it is available. You should also make at least two copies of each document you intend to introduce as evidence—one copy for your neighbor and one copy for the judge. You should organize and label all of your exhibits so that they are easy to locate and you will be able to introduce them in an orderly fashion as you present your testimony.

Obtaining Expert Witnesses

Depending on the issues involved in your case, you may need an expert witness to testify on your behalf. An expert witness is one who has special knowledge or experience in a particular area, who may be needed to explain to the judge or jury matters that are not easily understood by a layperson. For example, an arborist may be hired to explain why your 30-year old maple tree died when your neighbor cut the roots. An expert witness charges a fee for the time he or she spends working on your case.

Know Your Claim

It is crucial that you know all aspects of your claim. Go over your story and make note of the issues you must prove in order to prevail. You must be able to tell your side in a succinct and orderly manner without going into unnecessary or irrelevant details. It may be helpful to prepare a written outline, including: (1) why you brought the action; (2) what the defendant did or did not do; (3) why the defendant is at fault and why you are not at fault; and (4) the damages you suffered as a result of the defendant's actions or inaction. You must also anticipate the defense and be prepared to answer any questions your opponent or the court may ask.

Familiarize yourself with the small claims courtroom ahead of time. It is helpful to visit the courtroom and sit through several small claims hearings so you can get an idea of what to expect, where to sit, etc. If you know the name of the judge who will preside over your case, it is helpful to visit his or her courtroom during a small claims proceeding to get a sense of the judge's expectations, attitude and demeanor.

APPEARING FOR TRIAL

On the trial date, you should arrive at the courthouse before the calendar is called. The calendar is the list of cases being heard that day. You can find out from the clerk of the court the time of day the calendar is called. It is important that you arrive before your case is called or you risk having it dismissed, or having a default judgment entered against you if your neighbor made a claim or counterclaim against you.

When you arrive at the courthouse, you should check the court calendar to make sure your case is listed. The calendar is usually posted outside the courtroom door. In some jurisdictions, you must check in with the clerk of the court. When the calendar is ready to be called, the judge will enter the courtroom. The clerk will start reading the case names from the calendar in the order in which they appear. When you hear your case name, you should stand and state whether you are "plaintiff" or "defendant."

Prior to proceeding with the trial, the judge or clerk may make an effort to settle the case. If the parties are able to come to an agreement, the judge may read the details of the settlement into the court record. The judge may then dismiss the case without prejudice, which means if the parties do not consummate the settlement terms, either party can reopen the case and proceed to trial. In that case, in order to prevail, you may only need to show your neighbor violated the terms of the settlement agreement without having to present any other evidence.

If you do not appear in court for the trial, the case will usually be dismissed at that point. If your neighbor does not appear, you may request the court to enter a default judgment and schedule an inquest to determine damages, as discussed below.

PRESENTING YOUR CASE

Once the trial begins, you will present your case first. You will be sworn in by the court officer, and then you will be given the opportunity to tell your side of the story to the judge, who is the trier of both the facts and the law as it applies to the case. You are responsible for introducing all of the evidence that supports your claim.

After you finish testifying, your neighbor has the opportunity to "cross-examine" you with his or her own questions. The judge may also have questions for you. It is important to speak directly to the judge and avoid making any comments to your neighbor.

If you have any witnesses, they will be sworn in and testify next. You will ask your witnesses questions, and your neighbor will be able to cross-examine your witnesses. The judge may also follow up with questions for your witnesses.

You must be able to prove that you are entitled to the damages claimed in your complaint. The judge will not grant a judgment for any amount exceeding that which has been proven, even if your neighbor does not appear and you are awarded a default judgment.

You should prepare a written accounting of how you arrived at the damage amount, including calculations for items such as interest and court costs. Court costs are out-of-pockets costs which may include filing fees, process server fees, subpoena appearance fees, etc. You should bring receipts documenting all expenses for which you are seeking reimbursement.

After you and your witnesses have testified, and all your evidence has been submitted, your neighbor will be sworn in and will tell his or her version of the story. Your neighbor may also present evidence and witnesses on his or her behalf. The defendant should also be prepared to challenge your damage calculations. You may cross-examine your neighbor and your neighbor's witnesses, if any, and the judge may also follow up with questions.

It is important to maintain a calm demeanor while your neighbor and his or her witnesses are testifying, even if you believe they are incorrect or outright lying. You should never interrupt while another is testifying. You will get your chance to speak and clarify those issues you believe have been misrepresented. In addition, you should not interrupt the judge while he or she is speaking.

After both sides have told their stories, all witnesses have testified, and all evidence has been submitted, the judge will consider the evidence and make his or her decision. Depending on the jurisdiction, the judge may announce his or her decision in court following the trial, or the decision may be mailed to the parties.

DEFAULT JUDGMENT AND INQUEST

As set forth above, your neighbor fails to appear at trial, you may request a default judgment and inquest. An inquest is a hearing during which you present evidence in order to prove the claim and amount of damages. If the court determines that you have proven your case, a default judgment will be awarded in the amount sought. Your neighbor does not have the right to produce any evidence on his or her behalf at the inquest, if he or she attends.

APPENDIX 1:
SAMPLE WARNING LETTER

Date

John Smith
123 Main Street
Any City, Any State 12345

Dear John:

I am writing to follow up on our conversation concerning the use of your garage as an automobile body shop. As I pointed out, your customers' disabled cars are cluttering the street, and the noise from the machinery you use at all hours of the night in your garage is causing a disturbance and interferes with the peace and enjoyment of my property.

As I advised you, this is a residential area and local zoning laws prohibit using your home in this manner. I have attached a copy of the local zoning ordinance for your information. I hope that we can resolve this problem amicably, however, if you continue to use your garage in violation of the law, I will have no choice but to contact the proper authorities.

Thank you for your anticipated cooperation.

Sincerely,

Robert Jones

APPENDIX 2:
SAMPLE CONDOMINIUM FINE POLICY

NAME OF CONDOMINIUM ASSOCIATION:

RULES AND REGULATIONS

FINE POLICY - ASSESSMENT OF FINES

The violation by any Co-owner, occupant or guest of any of the provisions of the Condominium Documents (Master Deed, Bylaws or Rules and Regulations of the Association) shall be grounds for assessment by the Association, acting through its duly constituted Board of Directors, of monetary fines against the involved Co-owner.

Such Co-owner shall be deemed responsible for such violations whether they occur as a result of his personal actions or the actions of his family, guests, tenants or any other person admitted through such Co-owner to the Condominium Premises.

Upon any such violation being alleged by the Board, the following procedures will be followed:

A. Notice of the violation, including the Condominium Document provision violated, together with a description of the factual nature of the alleged offense set forth with such reasonable specificity as will place the Co-owner on notice as to the violation, shall be sent by first class mail, postage prepaid, or personally delivered to the representative of said Co-owner at the address as shown in the notice required to be filed with the Association pursuant to Article I, Section 3E, of the Restated Condominium Bylaws of [Name of Condominium Association].

B. The offending Co-owner shall be notified of a scheduled hearing before the Board at which the Co-owner may offer evidence in defense of the alleged violation. The appearance before the Board shall be at its next scheduled meeting, but in no event shall the Co-owner be required to appear less than 7 days from the date of the notice.

C. Failure to respond to the notice of violation or appear at the hearing constitutes a default.

D. Upon appearance by the Co-owner before the Board and presentation of evidence of defense, or, in the event of the Co-owner's default, the Board shall by majority vote of a quorum of the Board, decide whether a violation has occurred. The Board's decision is final.

SCHEDULE OF FINES

Upon violation of any of the provisions of the Condominium Documents and after default of the offending Co-owner or upon the decision of the Board as recited above, the following fines shall be levied:

First violation: Warning; no fine shall be levied.

Second Violation: A fine of $25.00 shall be levied.

Third Violation: A fine of $50.00 shall be levied.

Fourth Violation and Each Subsequent Violation: A fine of $100.00 shall be levied.

The Board of Directors, without the necessity of an amendment to the Restated Condominium Bylaws of [Name of Condominium Association], may make such changes in said fines or adopt alternative fines, including the indexing of such fines to the rate of inflation, in accordance with duly adopted Rules and Regulations promulgated in accordance with Article VI, Section 5 of the Restated Condominium Bylaws of [Name of Condominium Association]. For purposes of this Rule, the number of the violation (i.e., first, second, etc.) is determined with respect to the number of times that a Co-owner violates the same provision of the Condominium Documents, as long as that Co-owner may be an owner of a Unit or occupant of the Project, and is not based upon time or violations of entirely different provisions. In the case of continuing violations, a new violation will be deemed to occur each successive week during which a violation continues. Nothing in this Article shall be construed as to prevent the Association from pursuing any other remedy under the Condominium Documents and/or the [State] Condominium Act for such violations, or from combining a fine with any other remedy or requirement to redress any violation.

COLLECTION OF FINES

The fines levied pursuant to the above stated rules and regulations shall be assessed against the co-owner and shall be due and payable together with the regular monthly installment of the Annual Assessment next becoming due on the first day of the following month. Failure to pay the fine will subject the Co-owner to all liabilities set forth in the Condominium Documents, including without limitations, those described in Article II and Article XI of the Restated Condominium Bylaws of [Name of Condominium Association]. All unpaid amounts shall further constitute a lien on the Co-owner's unit, enforceable as set forth in Article II of the Restated Condominium Bylaws of [Name of Condominium Association].

APPENDIX 3:
SAMPLE FENCE HEIGHT REGULATION

VILLAGE OF MASSAPEQUA PARK, NEW YORK

CHAPTER 345: ZONING

§ 345-40. Fences and similar obstructions.

A. Erection restricted. No person shall erect in any residential district of the Village a solid fence, such as but not limited to a basket-weave-type fence, a solid board fence or any synthetic or metal solid fence that is greater than six feet in height or is before the front house setback; nor shall there be erected in such zone any fence more than 48 inches in height, excepting in the rear of the front line of the house, in which case the same shall be not more than six feet.

B. Corner plots.

(1) On corner plots, the front side shall be limited to nonopaque, not solid fences no higher than 48 inches. The street side (side yard) shall be entitled to a six-foot opaque (solid) fence, provided a minimum thirteen-foot setback from the property line is maintained. [Amended 3-27-2006 by L.L. No. 2-2006]

(2) Obstruction of view prohibited. On any corner plot on which a front or side yard is required, no wall, fence or structure shall be erected and no hedge, tree, shrub or other growth shall be maintained in such location within such required front or side yard space as to cause danger to traffic by obstruction of the view.

C. Location of posts and unfinished side facings. Any fence constructed in accordance with this section shall have the fence posts and/or unfinished side facings and/or horizontal and diagonal cross member pieces facing inward and located on the inside and/or that side of the property of the person who is erecting said fence. In the event that there is any question in reference to the above, it shall always be construed in favor of the adjoining property owner and against the person who is erecting said fence as to the location of said fence posts and/or unfinished side facings and/or horizontal and diagonal cross member pieces of the fence and/or any other item relating to the fence.

D. Permit required. No fence shall be erected within the Village in accordance with this section without first obtaining a permit from the Building Department of said Village.

E. Compliance required. No fence shall be permitted except as provided in this section or as authorized by the Zoning Board of Appeals after a public hearing.

F. The height of a fence shall be measured from the natural grade of the property at all points along the fence run. The height of the fence shall be the highest point of the fence measured at the natural grade. Man-made berms, retaining walls and other structures shall not be considered part of the natural grade. [Added 12-23-2002 by L.L. No. 10-2002]

G. All fences legally existing as of December 23, 2002, shall be permitted to remain as legal nonconforming fences. Legal nonconforming fences may be repaired and maintained. Any fence replaced or repaired to the extent of more than 50% of the existing fence must conform to § 345-40F. [Added 12-23-2002 by L.L. No. 10-2002]

APPENDIX 4:
COST-SHARING REQUEST LETTER –
BOUNDARY FENCE

Date

John Smith
123 Main Street
Any City, Any State 12345

    RE: Our Boundary Fence

Dear John:

I am writing to follow up on our conversation last week concerning the need to paint our boundary fence. As I pointed out, the paint is peeling and chipping, and in serious need of repair. State law requires that we share in the cost of repairing and maintaining the boundary fence. I have attached a copy of the law for your information.

I have taken the opportunity to obtain an estimate for the painting job. ABC Painters has agreed to paint the fence for $500. I have enclosed a copy of the estimate for your review. Your share of the cost would be $250.

Please contact me as soon as possible so that I can make an appointment with ABC Painters to begin the job.

Sincerely,

Robert Jones

APPENDIX 5:
DEMAND FOR REIMBURSEMENT OF
REPAIR COSTS – BOUNDARY FENCE

Date

John Smith
123 Main Street
Any City, Any State 12345

RE: Our Boundary Fence

Dear John:

In my letter dated [date], I requested that you share in the cost of painting our boundary fence, and provided you with an estimate. You ignored my letter and refused to speak with me about this matter, even though the fence was clearly in need of repair.

As you know, I hired ABC Painters to paint the fence. I have enclosed a copy of the paid bill in the amount of $500. I am requesting that you send me your share of the repair cost in the amount of $250.

Unfortunately, if you ignore my request for reimbursement, I will have no choice but to have this matter decided in small claims court. I don't believe this is in either of our best interests, therefore, I sincerely hope you comply with my request for reimbursement no later than [date].

Sincerely,

Robert Jones

APPENDIX 6:
SAMPLE FENCE VIEWER STATUTE

NEBRASKA REVISED STATUTES

§34-107. Controversy; determination by fence viewers; assignment; notice; procedure.

Upon receipt of a written request of any landowner, the county clerk shall assign three fence viewers from the panel of fence viewers appointed under §34-106 to determine any controversy arising under §§34-101 to 34-117. None of the fence viewers assigned shall be related by blood or marriage to the contending parties nor be financially interested in the outcome of the dispute. If the county clerk is unable to assign three fence viewers for any reason, the clerk shall notify the county sheriff who shall serve in place of the fence viewers or as one of the fence viewers, and all references to fence viewers in this section and §§34-104 to 34-111 shall be construed to mean the county sheriff if the sheriff is serving in place of the fence viewers. Before assigning the fence viewers, the clerk shall first require the landowner to show proof that notice has been given to adjoining landowners. Such notice shall be served upon any nonresident landowner by publication in a newspaper published in the county where the land is situated or by delivering a copy of the letter requesting the assignment of fence viewers to the occupant of such adjoining land or the landowner's agent in charge of such land. The fence viewers so assigned shall examine the premises and hear the allegations of the parties. The decision of any two of them shall be final upon the parties to such disputes and upon all parties holding under them.

§34-108. Controversy; determination; order; where filed; appeal.

The fence viewers shall determine by written order the obligations, rights, and duties of the respective parties in the controversy, shall assign to each landowner the part of the fence which the landowner shall erect, maintain, repair, or pay for, shall fix the value, including the costs of material and labor, and shall prescribe the time within which the erection, maintenance, or repair shall be completed or paid for. The fence viewers shall file the order forthwith in the office of the county clerk. Any person affected by an order of the fence viewers may appeal to the district court within 10 days after the date such order is filed.

APPENDIX 7:
SAMPLE METES AND BOUNDS PROPERTY DESCRIPTION

PROPERTY OWNER:

LEGAL DESCRIPTION OF PROPERTY LOCATED AT _____**, IN THE CITY OF** _____**,** _____**County, State of** _____**, and more particularly described as follows:**

Beginning at a point on the northeasterly corner of the intersection of North Street and West Road, running thence northerly along West Road 300 feet, thence easterly parallel to North Street 250 feet; thence southerly parallel to West Road 300 feet; thence westerly along South Street 250 feet to the point of beginning.

APPENDIX 8:
PENNSYLVANIA ADVERSE POSSESSION STATUTE

UNCONSOLIDATED PENNSYLVANIA STATUTES

TITLE 68: REAL AND PERSONAL PROPERTY

§ 81. Statement of claim under statute of limitations, by claimant out of possession.

Every person who now has or shall hereafter acquire, or does or shall claim to have acquired, title to any real estate by twenty-one years' adverse possession, under the provisions of the act of twenty-sixth March, one thousand seven hundred and eighty-five, and the several supplements thereto, and shall not be in the possession of the said real estate, shall, within six months from the time of withdrawing from or being out of the said possession, file in the recorder's office of the county where the said real estate is situate a written statement of his claim, by him subscribed and sworn to, in substance as follows, viz.:

§ 82. Form of statement.

I, A.B., (the name of the party claimant), of _____, in the county of _____ and state of _____, (or as the case may be) do hereby affirm and declare that I have acquired title in fee, by twenty-one years' adverse possession, to the following described land, situate in _____, in the county of _____, and state of Pennsylvania, viz.: (Here insert a full and complete description of the land claimed, by metes and bounds, or other sufficient designation). Adverse entry was made upon the said land by me on or about the _____ day of _____, Anno Domini _____, and continued until about the _____ day of _____, Anno Domini _____, (or, where the possession of the claimant is tacked on to that of others who have preceded him, it should be stated as follows:

Adverse entry was made upon said lands by _____ on or about the _____ day of _____, Anno Domini _____, who continued in possession until about the _____ day of _____, Anno Domini _____, and was succeeded therein by _____, who continued in possession until about the _____ day of _____, Anno Domini _____, and was succeeded therein by me, who continued in possession until about the _____ day of _____ Anno Domini _____). At the time of the said entry C.D. (Naming some person or persons in the line of the existing paper or legal title, as nearly as may be the real owner of said lands at the time of such entry), was the owner or reputed owner of the said land, and I claim adversely to him (or them).

Witness my hand, this _____ day of _____, Anno Domini _____.

(signed)

A.B.

§ 83. Executor, trustee, guardian, etc., may make statement; effect.

The said statement of claim shall be made by an executor, invested with the title or charged with the care and management of real estate for the estate which he represents; by a trustee, for his cestuis que trustent; for an infant, by his guardian or next friend; and for a lunatic or inebriate, by his committee. It may also be made by one heir, or devisee, for himself and his co-heirs or co-devisees; and by one joint tenant or tenant in common, for himself and his co-tenants; and, being so made, shall operate in favor of each of the said heirs, devisees, joint tenants, or tenants in common; but no such statement shall preclude any other of such heirs, devisees or co-tenants from making and recording a statement on his own behalf, according to the facts as he claims them to be.

§ 84. Statement must be subscribed and sworn to; form of oath.

The said statement shall be subscribed and sworn to before some officer competent to administer oaths and affirmations, who shall attest the same substantially as follows, viz.: County of _____, state of _____ss. Be it remembered, that on the _____, day of _____, Anno Domini _____, before me, the subscriber, (here designate the title of the attesting officer) personally appeared A.B. (naming the claimant), who, having been duly sworn, (or affirmed) did declare and say that the facts set forth in his foregoing statement of claim are true, as he verily believes.

Witness my hand and official seal, the day and year aforesaid. X.Y., Notary Public (or as the case may be). (L.S.)

§ 85. Statement to be recorded same as deeds; effect.

The said statement of claim, on being filed in the recorder's office of the proper county, shall be recorded and indexed as though it were a deed or conveyance from the person named therein as the owner or reputed owner at the time of the adverse entry, as grantor, to the claimant or claimants, as grantees; and when so entered for record and indexed it shall be constructive notice of the said claim.

§ 86. Claim invalid as against purchaser without notice if not recorded.

Unless a statement of claim be made and recorded as herein provided, no title to lands by twenty-one years' adverse possession, as aforesaid, shall avail against any purchaser, mortgagee, or judgement creditor for value, without notice, his heirs and assigns, except the claimant be in possession of such lands at the time of such purchase.

§ 87. Act to apply to existing claims.

Any person claiming to have heretofore acquired title to lands by twenty-one years' adverse possession, under the statute, and not now being in possession of the same, shall record his claim, in the manner hereinbefore provided, within six months after the passage of this act, or be barred as aforesaid thereby.

§ 88. Act not to apply to claims adverse to the Commonwealth.

Nothing contained in this act shall be construed to give any title to any lands by a claim of title adverse to that of the Commonwealth of Pennsylvania, and no claim of title adverse to the Commonwealth of Pennsylvania shall be made or recorded under the provisions of this act.

PENNSYLVANIA CONSOLIDATED STATUTES

TITLE 42: JUDICIARY AND JUDICIAL PROCEDURE

PART VI. ACTIONS, PROCEEDINGS AND OTHER MATTERS GENERALLY

SUBCHAPTER B. CIVIL ACTIONS AND PROCEEDINGS

§ 5530. Twenty-one year limitation

(a) General rule.—The following actions and proceedings must be commenced within 21 years:

1. An action for the possession of real property.

APPENDIX 9:
COVENANT OF QUIET ENJOYMENT OF LEASED PREMISES

Landlord hereby covenants, warrants and represents to Tenant that, upon payment of the rent and observing all provisions herein required by this Lease, Tenant shall have the right to quietly and peaceably have, hold and enjoy the premises during the term set forth in the Lease.

APPENDIX 10:
NOISE ORDINANCE – CITY OF BUFFALO, NEW YORK

CHAPTER 293: NOISE

§ 293-1. Findings; intent.

The Common Council determines that the creation of excessive and unreasonable noise within the city limits of Buffalo is a detriment to the comfort, convenience, safety, health and welfare of the citizens of the city and that persons within the city are entitled to have maintained noise levels which are not a detriment to life, health, welfare and enjoyment of property. Therefore, it intends hereby to prohibit all excessive and unreasonable noise from all sources subject to its police power in order to preserve, protect and promote health, safety and welfare and the peace, quiet, comfort and repose of persons within the city.

§ 293-2. Definitions.

As used in this chapter, the following terms shall have the meanings indicated:

AMBIENT NOISE—The all-encompassing noise associated with a given environment, being usually a composite of sounds from near and far.

DAY—The hours between 7:00 a.m. and 9:00 p.m., except Fridays and Saturdays, when the evening hours shall be 11:00 p.m.

DECIBEL—A standard unit of acoustic measurement having a zero-reference of two ten-thousandths (0.0002) microbar.

IMPULSIVE NOISE—A noise of short duration.

NOISE-RATING NUMBER—The criteria established in the noise-rating curves of the International Standards Organization.

OCTAVE BAND—The range of sound frequencies divided into octaves in order to classify sound according to pitch.

PERSON—Any individual, firm, corporation, association, club, partnership, society or any other form of association or organization.

PUBLIC RIGHT-OF-WAY—Any street, sidewalk or alley or similar place which is owned or controlled by the City of Buffalo, including but not limited to walks, regardless of designation.

PUBLIC SPACE—Any real property or structure thereon which is owned, controlled or leased by the City of Buffalo.

PURE TONE—A sound having a single pitch.

REAL PROPERTY BOUNDARY—An imaginary line along the ground surface and its vertical extension, which separates the real property owned by one person from that owned by another person or from any public right-of way or from any public space.

SOUND—An oscillation in pressure, partial velocity or other physical parameter in a medium with internal forces that cause compression and rarefaction of the medium.

SOUND-LEVEL METER—An instrument, including a microphone, an amplifier, an output meter and frequency-weighting networks, used for the measurement of sound in a specified manner and calibrated in decibels.

SOUND REPRODUCTION DEVICE—Any device, instrument, mechanism, equipment or apparatus for the amplification of any sounds from any radio, phonograph, stereo, tape player, musical instrument, television, loudspeaker or other sound-making or sound-producing device or any device or apparatus for the reproduction or amplification of the human voice or other sound.

UNREASONABLE NOISES—Any noise which is defined in § 293-4 or § 293-5.

VEHICLE—Any land conveyance, self-propelled or propelled by an internal source.

VESSEL—Includes every description of watercraft used or capable of being used as a means of transportation in, on or upon water, including but not limited to nondisplacement craft and seaplanes.

WITHIN THE COMMERCIAL AREA—Sound emanating from a source within the commercial area. Sound shall not be considered "within the commercial area" if it is projected into, heard or felt in a residential area, and such sound shall be considered to be within the residential area and governed by the rules relating thereto.

ZONING DISTRICT—A district established in accordance with Chapter 511, Zoning, of this Code.

§ 293-4. Unreasonable noise prohibited.

It shall be unlawful for any person to make, continue, cause to be made or permit to be made any unreasonable noise within the geographical boundaries of the City of Buffalo or within those areas over which the city has jurisdiction. The determination as to the existence of unreasonable noise may be established either by the specific acts considered to be unreasonable noise enumerated within § 293-4 or by the measurements exceeding the limitations set forth in § 293-5.

§ 293-4. Specific acts constituting unreasonable noise.

The following acts and the causes thereof are declared to be in violation of this chapter and to constitute unreasonable noise:

A. The use of any sound-reproduction device outside a structure either on private property or on a public right-of way or public space at any time within the residential areas or within the commercial areas which, by causing noise, annoys or disturbs the quiet, comfort or repose of a reasonable person of normal sensitivities. This provision shall not be construed to prohibit public performances being conducted in accordance with the provisions of a special permit granted by the city.

B. The use of any sound-reproduction device inside a structure in such a manner as to result in the sound or any part thereof from such apparatus to be projected therefrom outside of the structure or out of doors at any time within the residential areas or during night hours in the commercial areas whereby the sound can be audibly heard more than one hundred (100) feet from the real property boundary line from which the noise emanates. Sound which crosses any real property boundary shall be deemed to be projected within the meaning of this chapter. Nothing within Subsections A and B herein shall be construed to prevent the operation of any such apparatus by any person within any building or structure, provided that the sound therefrom or any part thereof is not projected outside of any building or out of doors, or to prohibit the use of any apparatus with a personal earphone so that the sound therefrom or any part thereof is not audible to persons other than the user of the earphone.

C. The operation of any sound-reproduction device on a vessel so that the sound therefrom is audible on land, which annoys or disturbs the quiet, comfort or repose of a reasonable person of normal sensitivities.

D. The use and operation of any sound-reproduction device in a vehicle which would constitute a threat to the safety of pedestrians or vehicle operators or where conditions of overcrowding or street repair or other physical conditions are such that the use of a sound reproduction device would deprive the public of the right to the safe, comfortable, convenient and peaceful enjoyment of a public street, park or place for public purpose and would constitute a threat to the safety and welfare of the public.

E. The operation of any sound-reproduction device within five hundred (500) feet of any school, church, health-care facility, clinic or courthouse while the same is in session or conducting business therein so as to interfere with the functions of such activities.

F. The operation of any sound-reproduction device within five hundred (500) feet of any hospital, nursing home or similar facility whereby the sound emanating from the device can be audibly heard within the building or structure therein and so as to interfere with the functions of such activities or disturb or annoy the patients in the activity, provided that conspicuous signs are displayed indicating the presence of the zone.

G. Yelling, shouting or hooting at any time or place so as to annoy or disturb the quiet, comfort and repose of a reasonable person of normal sensitivities.

H. The use of any drum, loudspeaker or other instrument or device for the purpose of attracting attention to any business, which annoys or disturbs the quiet, comfort and repose of a reasonable person of normal sensitivities.

I. Construction activity.

(1) The performance or engagement in construction work, building, excavating, hoisting, grading, demolishing, dredging or pneumatic hammering within the limits of the city between the hours of 9:00 p.m. and 7:00 a.m. that causes sound which annoys or disturbs a reasonable person of normal sensitivities in a residential real property zone, except for emergency work of public service utilities or as otherwise provided in Subsection I (b) herein.

(2) Any person desiring to engage in the aforesaid activity beyond the stated hours of limitation, based upon cases of urgent necessity or upon the interests of public health, safety and convenience, may apply to the Commissioner of Public Works for a special permit allowing such activity. The permits, if granted, shall be limited to a period of up to three (3) days' duration but

may be renewed for additional periods of up to three (3) days each if the emergency or need continues. In the issuance of these permits, the Commissioner of Public Works shall weigh all facts and circumstances and shall determine whether the reasons given for the urgent necessity are valid and reasonable, whether the public health, safety and ultimate convenience will be protected or better served by granting the permit requested and whether the manner and amount of loss or inconvenience to the party in interest imposes a significant hardship.

J. The sounding of any horn, security alarm or other auditory signaling device in any vehicle, vessel, engine, machine or stationary boiler for period of time longer than five (5) minutes, except as required by law or to provide a warning signal during use thereof. This provision shall not be construed to prohibit the use and operation of a signal device in an emergency vehicle.

K. The operation of a vehicle without an adequate muffler or exhaust system to prevent any unreasonable noise in violation of the Vehicle and Traffic Law § 375, Subdivision 31.

L. The use and operation of any lawn maintenance device, including mowers, edgers, trimmers and power-driven hedge shears, between the hours of 9:00 p.m. and 7:00 a.m. that causes sound that annoys or disturbs a reasonable person of normal sensitivities in a residential real property zone. This provision does not apply to the operation such equipment on golf courses.

M. The use and operation of air conditioners, snowblowers or other mechanical devices which cause noise that annoys or disturbs the quiet, comfort or repose of a reasonable person of normal sensitivities, except upon cases of urgent necessity or upon the interests of public health, safety and convenience. This provision shall not be construed to prohibit the use and operation of city, county, state or other governmental equipment otherwise in compliance with the provisions of this chapter.

N. The keeping of any animal or bird, which causes noise that, annoys or disturbs the quiet, comfort or repose of a reasonable person of normal sensitivities. This provision shall not apply to public zoos.

O. Any other excessive or unreasonable noise which either annoys, disturbs, injures or endangers the comfort, repose, health, peace or safety of a reasonable person of normal sensitivities, except that the enumerated provisions of Subsections A through N of this section shall govern and regulate the actions and activities therein prohibited, and nothing contained in this Subsection O shall apply to those actions and activities set forth in Subsections A through N of this section.

§ 293-5. Additional guidelines to determine unreasonable noise. [Amended 10-2-1990, effective 10-11-1990]

A. The subject noise must exceed ambient noise by five (5) decibels or more in any octave band to be declared excessive or unreasonable.

B. Sound projecting from one use district into another use district having a lower noise-level limit shall not exceed the limits of the district into which it is projected.

§ 293-6. Methods of measurement.

A. Noise measurements shall be made with a sound-level meter and compatible octave band analyzer manufactured according to the specification of the American National Standards Institute, USA Standard Specification for General Purpose Sound Level Meters (51.4-1971) and Preferred Center Frequencies for Acoustical Measurements (51.6-1960) or any subsequent nationally adopted standard superseding the above standards.

B. Except where impractical, sound measurements shall be made from the specific position of the complainant at the premises from which noise complaints are received and shall be made at a height of at least three (3) feet above the ground and three (3) feet away from walls, barriers, obstructions or other sound-reflective surfaces. Where the nature of the noise permits, the slow response setting shall be used to obtain the noise level on the sound-level meter. The sound analysis curve shall be plotted in decibels upon the noise-rating numbers chart, and the highest portion of the curve in any octave band above a noise-rating curve shall be the noise-rating number for the measurement. The average curve of several noise measurements may be used to plot the sound analysis curve.

C. When detailed sound analysis measurement cannot be made, a measurement of the noise using the A scale of a standard sound-level meter may be made, and the noise-rating number shall be determined by this measurement minus eight (8) decibels.

§ 293-7. Penalty for offenses. [Added 11-12-1996, effective 11-25-1996]

Any person violating the provisions of this chapter may be liable for penalties as prescribed in Chapter 137, Article I, of this Code.

APPENDIX 11:
STATE SEX OFFENDER REGISTRATION WEBSITES

STATE	WEBSITE
ALABAMA	http://www.dps.state.al.us
ALASKA	http://www.dps.state.ak.us/nsorcr/asp
ARIZONA	http://www.azsexoffender.com/
ARKANSAS	http://www.acic.org/Registration/index.htm
CALIFORNIA	http://www.meganslaw.ca.gov/
COLORADO	http://sor.state.co.us/default.asp
CONNECTICUT	http://www.state.ct.us/dps
DELAWARE	http://www.state.de.us/dsp/sexoff/index.htm
DISTRICT OF COLUMBIA	http://www.mpdc.dc.gov
FLORIDA	http://www.fdle.state.fl.us/index.asp?/sexual_predators/
GEORGIA	http://www.Georgia-Sex-Offenders.com
HAWAII	http://pahoehoe.ehawaii.gov/sexoff/index.html
IOWA	http://www.iowasexoffenders.com
IDAHO	http://www.isp.state.id.us/identification/sex_offender/index.html
ILLINOIS	http://www.isp.state.il.us/sor/frames.htm
INDIANA	http://www.state.in.us/serv/cji_sor
KANSAS	http://www.accesskansas.org/kbi/ro.htm
KENTUCKY	http://kspsor.state.ky.us/
LOUISIANA	http://www.lasocpr.lsp.org/socpr/
MAINE	http://www4.informe.org/sor/
MARYLAND	http://www.dpscs.state.md.us/sor/
MASSACHUSETTS	http://www.state.ma.us/sorb/community.htm
MICHIGAN	http://www.mipsor.state.mi.us
MINNESOTA	http://www.doc.state.mn.us/level3/level3.asp
MISSISSIPPI	http://www.sor.mdps.state.ms.us/

STATE	WEBSITE
MISSOURI	http://www.mshp.dps.missouri.gov/MSHPWeb/PatrolDivisions/
MONTANA	http://www.doj.mt.gov/svor/
NEBRASKA	http://www.nsp.state.ne.us/sor/find.cfm
NEVADA	http://www.nvsexoffenders.gov
NEW HAMPSHIRE	http://oit.nh.gov/nsor/
NEW JERSEY	http://www.state.nj.us/lps/dcj/megan/meghome.htm
NEW MEXICO	http://www.nmsexoffender.dps.state.nm.us/
NEW YORK	http://criminaljustice.state.ny.us/nsor/index.htm
NORTH CAROLINA	http://sbi.jus.state.nc.us/DOJHAHT/SOR/default.htm
NORTH DAKOTA	http://www.ndsexoffender.com
OHIO	http://www.ag.state.oh.us
OKLAHOMA	http://docapp8.doc.state.ok.us
OREGON	http://www.co.benton.or.us/sheriff/corrections/bccc/sonote/
PENNSYLVANIA	http://www.psp.state.pa.us
SOUTH CAROLINA	http://www.sled.state.sc.us
SOUTH DAKOTA	http://www.sddci.com/administration/id/sexoffender/index.asp
TENNESSEE	http://www.ticic.state.tn.us/
TEXAS	http://records.txdps.state.tx.us/
UTAH	http://corrections.utah.gov/community/sexoffenders/ Email: registry@udc.state.ut.us
VERMONT	http://www.dps.state.vt.us/cjs/s_registry.htm (Information only)
VIRGINIA	http://sex-offender.vsp.state.va.us/cool-ICE/
WASHINGTON	http://ml.waspc.org
WEST VIRGINIA	http://www.wvstatepolice.com
WISCONSIN	http://offender.doc.state.wi.us/public/
WYOMING	http://attorneygeneral.state.wy.us/dci/so/so_registration.html

APPENDIX 12:
AGREEMENT TO MEDIATE DISPUTE

The named parties hereby agree to submit the following dispute for mediation under the applicable Rules of the American Arbitration Association.

PARTIES:

Claimant: [Name and Address]

Respondent: [Name and Address]

THE NATURE OF THE DISPUTE: [DESCRIBE DISPUTE]

THE CLAIM OR RELIEF SOUGHT [Describe relief sought, including the amount, if any]:

PLACE OF MEDIATION: [SELECTION LOCATION]

SIGNATURES OF PARTIES:

BY: _____

Name of Party:

Address:

Telephone:

Fax:

BY: _____

Name of Party:

Address:

Telephone:

Fax:

APPENDIX 13:
REGIONAL OFFICES OF THE AMERICAN ARBITRATION ASSOCIATION
(AAA)

REGIONAL OFFICE	AREAS COVRED	ADDRESS	TELEPHONE NUMBER	FAX NUMBER
Arizona	Arizona, Nevada, and New Mexico	3200 North Central Avenue, Suite 2100, Phoenix, AZ 85012-2441	602-734-9333	602-230-2151
California	Los Angeles, Inyo, Kern, Kings, Los Angeles, San Bernardino, San Luis Obispo, Santa Barbara and Ventura Counties	725 South Figueroa Street, Suite 2400, Los Angeles, CA 90017	213-362-1900	213-623-9134
California – San Diego	Imperial, Orange and San Diego Counties	600 B Street, Suite 1450, San Diego, CA 92101-4586	619-239-3051	619-239-3807
California - San Francisco	Northern California and Hawaii	One Sansome Street, 16th Floor, San Francisco, CA 94101-4449	415-981-3901	415-781-8426

REGIONAL OFFICE	AREAS COVRED	ADDRESS	TELEPHONE NUMBER	FAX NUMBER
Colorado	Colorado, Idaho, Montana, Utah and Wyoming	1675 Broadway, Suite 2550, Denver, CO 80202-4602	303-831-0823	303-832-3626
Florida – Miami	South Florida (including Hardee, Highlands, Manatee, Okeechobee and St. Lucie Counties) and the Caribbean	Bank of America Tower at International Place, 100 SE 2nd Street, Suite 2300, Miami, FL 33131-2808	305-358-7777	305-358-4931
Florida – Orlando	North Florida	315 East Robinson Street, Suite 290, Orlando, FL 32801	407-648-1185	407-649-8668
Georgia	Alabama, Georgia and Tennessee	2200 Century Parkway, Suite 300, Atlanta, GA 30345-3203	404-325-0101	404-325-8034
Illinois	Illinois and Wisconsin	225 North Michigan Avenue, Suite 1840, hicago, IL 60601-7601	312-616-6560	312-819-0404
Louisiana	Louisiana and Mississippi	2725 Energy Centre, 1100 Poydras Street, New Orleans, LA 70163-2701	504-522-8781	504-561-8041
Massachusetts	Connecticut, Maine, Massachusetts, New Hampshire, Rhode Island and Vermont	One Center Plaza, Suite 300, 3rd Floor, Boston, MA 02108	617-451-6600	617-451-0763
Michigan	Michigan	27777 Franklin Road, Suite 1150, 11th Floor, Southfield, MI 48034	248-352-5500	248-352-3147

REGIONAL OFFICE	AREAS COVRED	ADDRESS	TELEPHONE NUMBER	FAX NUMBER
Minnesota	Minnesota, North Dakota and South Dakota	700 U.S. Bank Plaza, 200 South Sixth Street, Minneapolis, MN 55402-1092	612-332-6545	612-342-2334
Missouri	Iowa, Kansas, Missouri and Nebraska	100 N. Broadway, Suite 1820, St. Louis, MO 63102	314-621-7175	314-621-3730
New Jersey	New Jersey	220 Davidson Avenue, 1st Floor, Somerset, NJ 08873-4159	732-560-9560	732-560-8850
New York	New York	1633 Broadway, Floor 10, New York, NY 10019-6708	212-484-3266	212-307-4387
North Carolina	North Carolina and South Carolina	200 South College Street, Suite 1800, Charlotte, NC 28202	704-347-0200	704-347-2804
Ohio	Indiana, Kentucky and Ohio	250 East Fifth Street, Suite 330, Cincinnati, OH 45202-4173	513-241-8434	513-241-8437
Pennsylvania	Delaware, Pennsylvania and West Virginia	230 South Broad Street, Floor 12, Philadelphia, PA 19102-4199	215-732-5260	215-732-5002
Texas – Dallas	Arkansas, Okalahoma and in Texas, All Cities North of and Including Waco	1770 Two Galleria Tower, 13455 Noel Road, Dallas, TX 75240-6636	972-774-6947	972-503-1049
Texas – Houston	All Cities in a Line South of and Including El Paso to Austin to Nacogdoches	1331 Lamar, Suite 1180, Houston, TX 77010	713-739-1302	713-739-1702

REGIONAL OFFICE	AREAS COVRED	ADDRESS	TELEPHONE NUMBER	FAX NUMBER
Washington	Alaska, Oregon and Washington	701 Pike Street, Suite 950, Seattle, WA 98101-4111	206-622-6435	206-343-5679
Washington, D.C.	Maryland, Virginia and Washington, D.C.	1776 Eye Street, NW, Suite 850, Washington, D.C. 20006	202-739-8280	202-222-7095

APPENDIX 14:
MODEL STANDARDS OF CONDUCT FOR MEDIATORS

STANDARD I. SELF-DETERMINATION

A. A mediator shall conduct a mediation based on the principle of party self-determination. Self-determination is the act of coming to a voluntary, uncoerced decision in which each party makes free and informed choices as to process and outcome. Parties may exercise self-determination at any stage of a mediation, including mediator selection, process design, participation in or withdrawal from the process, and outcomes.

1. Although party self-determination for process design is a fundamental principle of mediation practice, a mediator may need to balance such party self-determination with a mediator's duty to conduct a quality process in accordance with these Standards.

2. A mediator cannot personally ensure that each party has made free and informed choices to reach particular decisions, but, where appropriate, a mediator should make the parties aware of the importance of consulting other professionals to help them make informed choices.

B. A mediator shall not undermine party self-determination by any party for reasons such as higher settlement rates, egos, increased fees, or outside pressures from court personnel, program administrators, provider organizations, the media or others.

STANDARD II. IMPARTIALITY

A. A mediator shall decline a mediation if the mediator cannot conduct it in an impartial manner. Impartiality means freedom from favoritism, bias or prejudice.

B. A mediator shall conduct a mediation in an impartial manner and avoid conduct that gives the appearance of partiality.

1. A mediator should not act with partiality or prejudice based on any participant's personal characteristics, background, values and beliefs, or performance at a mediation, or any other reason.

2. A mediator should neither give nor accept a gift, favor, loan or other item of value that raises a question as to the mediator's actual or perceived impartiality.

3. A mediator may accept or give de minimis gifts or incidental items or services that are provided to facilitate a mediation or respect cultural norms so long as such practices do not raise questions as to a mediator's actual or perceived impartiality.

C. If at any time a mediator is unable to conduct a mediation in an impartial manner, the mediator shall withdraw.

STANDARD III. CONFLICTS OF INTEREST

A. A mediator shall avoid a conflict of interest or the appearance of a conflict of interest during and after a mediation. A conflict of interest can arise from involvement by a mediator with the subject matter of the dispute or from any relationship between a mediator and any mediation participant, whether past or present, personal or professional, that reasonably raises a question of a mediator's impartiality.

B. A mediator shall make a reasonable inquiry to determine whether there are any facts that a reasonable individual would consider likely to create a potential or actual conflict of interest for a mediator. A mediator's actions necessary to accomplish a reasonable inquiry into potential conflicts of interest may vary based on practice context.

C. A mediator shall disclose, as soon as practicable, all actual and potential conflicts of interest that are reasonably known to the mediator and could reasonably be seen as raising a question about the mediator's impartiality. After disclosure, if all parties agree, the mediator may proceed with the mediation.

D. If a mediator learns any fact after accepting a mediation that raises a question with respect to that mediator's service creating a potential or actual conflict of interest, the mediator shall disclose it as quickly as practicable. After disclosure, if all parties agree, the mediator may proceed with the mediation.

E. If a mediator's conflict of interest might reasonably be viewed as undermining the integrity of the mediation, a mediator shall withdraw from or decline to proceed with the mediation regardless of the expressed desire or agreement of the parties to the contrary.

F. Subsequent to a mediation, a mediator shall not establish another relationship with any of the participants in any matter that would raise questions about the integrity of the mediation. When a mediator develops personal or professional relationships with parties, other individuals or organizations following a mediation in which they were involved, the mediator should consider factors such as time elapsed following the mediation, the nature of the relationships established, and services offered when determining whether the relationships might create a perceived or actual conflict of interest.

STANDARD IV. COMPETENCE

A. A mediator shall mediate only when the mediator has the necessary competence to satisfy the reasonable expectations of the parties.

1. Any person may be selected as a mediator, provided that the parties are satisfied with the mediator's competence and qualifications. Training, experience in mediation, skills, cultural understandings and other qualities are often necessary for mediator competence. A person who offers to serve as a mediator creates the expectation that the person is competent to mediate effectively.

2. A mediator should attend educational programs and related activities to maintain and enhance the mediator's knowledge and skills related to mediation.

3. A mediator should have available for the parties' information relevant to the mediator's training, education, experience and approach to conducting a mediation.

B. If a mediator, during the course of a mediation determines that the mediator cannot conduct the mediation competently, the mediator shall discuss that determination with the parties as soon as is practicable and take appropriate steps to address the situation, including, but not limited to, withdrawing or requesting appropriate assistance.

C. If a mediator's ability to conduct a mediation is impaired by drugs, alcohol, medication or otherwise, the mediator shall not conduct the mediation.

STANDARD V. CONFIDENTIALITY

A. A mediator shall maintain the confidentiality of all information obtained by the mediator in mediation, unless otherwise agreed to by the parties or required by applicable law.

1. If the parties to a mediation agree that the mediator may disclose information obtained during the mediation, the mediator may do so.

2. A mediator should not communicate to any non-participant information about how the parties acted in the mediation. A mediator may report, if required, whether parties appeared at a scheduled mediation and whether or not the parties reached a resolution.

3. If a mediator participates in teaching, research or evaluation of mediation, the mediator should protect the anonymity of the parties and abide by their reasonable expectations regarding confidentiality.

B. A mediator who meets with any persons in private session during a mediation shall not convey directly or indirectly to any other person, any information that was obtained during that private session without the consent of the disclosing person.

C. A mediator shall promote understanding among the parties of the extent to which the parties will maintain confidentiality of information they obtain in a mediation.

D. Depending on the circumstance of a mediation, the parties may have varying expectations regarding confidentiality that a mediator should address. The parties may make their own rules with respect to confidentiality, or the accepted practice of an individual mediator or institution may dictate a particular set of expectations.

STANDARD VI. QUALITY OF THE PROCESS

A. A mediator shall conduct a mediation in accordance with these Standards and in a manner that promotes diligence, timeliness, safety, presence of the appropriate participants, party participation, procedural fairness, party competency and mutual respect among all participants.

1. A mediator should agree to mediate only when the mediator is prepared to commit the attention essential to an effective mediation.

2. A mediator should only accept cases when the mediator can satisfy the reasonable expectation of the parties concerning the timing of a mediation.

3. The presence or absence of persons at a mediation depends on the agreement of the parties and the mediator. The parties and mediator

may agree that others may be excluded from particular sessions or from all sessions.

4. A mediator should promote honesty and candor between and among all participants, and a mediator shall not knowingly misrepresent any material fact or circumstance in the course of a mediation.

5. The role of a mediator differs substantially from other professional roles. Mixing the role of a mediator and the role of another profession is problematic and thus, a mediator should distinguish between the roles. A mediator may provide information that the mediator is qualified by training or experience to provide, only if the mediator can do so consistent with these Standards.

6. A mediator shall not conduct a dispute resolution procedure other than mediation but label it mediation in an effort to gain the protection of rules, statutes, or other governing authorities pertaining to mediation.

7. A mediator may recommend, when appropriate, that parties consider resolving their dispute through arbitration, counseling, neutral evaluation or other processes.

8. A mediator shall not undertake an additional dispute resolution role in the same matter without the consent of the parties. Before providing such service, a mediator shall inform the parties of the implications of the change in process and obtain their consent to the change. A mediator who undertakes such role assumes different duties and responsibilities that may be governed by other standards.

9. If a mediation is being used to further criminal conduct, a mediator should take appropriate steps including, if necessary, postponing, withdrawing from or terminating the mediation.

10. If a party appears to have difficulty comprehending the process, issues, or settlement options, or difficulty participating in a mediation, the mediator should explore the circumstances and potential accommodations, modifications or adjustments that would make possible the party's capacity to comprehend, participate and exercise self-determination.

B. If a mediator is made aware of domestic abuse or violence among the parties, the mediator shall take appropriate steps including, if necessary, postponing, withdrawing from or terminating the mediation.

C. If a mediator believes that participant conduct, including that of the mediator, jeopardizes conducting a mediation consistent with these Standards, a mediator shall take appropriate steps including, if necessary, postponing, withdrawing from or terminating the mediation.

STANDARD VII. ADVERTISING AND SOLICITATION

A. A mediator shall be truthful and not misleading when advertising, soliciting or otherwise communicating the mediator's qualifications, experience, services and fees.

1. A mediator should not include any promises as to outcome in communications, including business cards, stationery, or computer-based communications.

2. A mediator should only claim to meet the mediator qualifications of a governmental entity or private organization if that entity or organization has a recognized procedure for qualifying mediators and it grants such status to the mediator.

B. A mediator shall not solicit in a manner that gives an appearance of partiality for or against a party or otherwise undermines the integrity of the process.

C. A mediator shall not communicate to others, in promotional materials or through other forms of communication, the names of persons served without their permission.

STANDARD VIII. FEES AND OTHER CHARGES

A. A mediator shall provide each party or each party's representative true and complete information about mediation fees, expenses and any other actual or potential charges that may be incurred in connection with a mediation.

1. If a mediator charges fees, the mediator should develop them in light of all relevant factors, including the type and complexity of the matter, the qualifications of the mediator, the time required and the rates customary for such mediation services.

2. A mediator's fee arrangement should be in writing unless the parties request otherwise.

B. A mediator shall not charge fees in a manner that impairs a mediator's impartiality.

1. A mediator should not enter into a fee agreement which is contingent upon the result of the mediation or amount of the settlement.

2. While a mediator may accept unequal fee payments from the parties, a mediator should not use fee arrangements that adversely impact the mediator's ability to conduct a mediation in an impartial manner.

STANDARD IX. ADVANCEMENT OF MEDIATION PRACTICE

A. A mediator should act in a manner that advances the practice of mediation. A mediator promotes this Standard by engaging in some or all of the following:

1. Fostering diversity within the field of mediation.

2. Striving to make mediation accessible to those who elect to use it, including providing services at a reduced rate or on a pro bono basis as appropriate.

3. Participating in research when given the opportunity, including obtaining participant feedback when appropriate.

4. Participating in outreach and education efforts to assist the public in developing an improved understanding of, and appreciation for, mediation.

5. Assisting newer mediators through training, mentoring and networking.

B. A mediator should demonstrate respect for differing points of view within the field, seek to learn from other mediators and work together with other mediators to improve the profession and better serve people in conflict.

APPENDIX 15:
SETTLEMENT AGREEMENT AND GENERAL RELEASE OF CLAIMS

AGREEMENT made as of the ____ day of _____, ____ between JOHN SMITH, residing at _____ (hereinafter "Smith") and JANE DOE, _____ (hereinafter, "Doe").

IN CONSIDERATION of the mutual covenants and agreements herein contained, the parties hereto agree as follows:

1. In full, final and complete settlement of any and all claims, as provided herein, and upon execution of this Agreement by the parties, Doe agrees to pay Smith the total sum of Two Thousand ($2,000) Dollars by check, subject to collection.

2. Smith hereby releases and forever discharges Doe from any and all claims arising out of or in connection with any acts or omissions by Doe.

3. Specifically, Smith releases Doe from any and all claims resulting from water damage to Smith's basement which occurred on _____, ____ as a result of a broken drain pipe on Doe's property which flooded Smith's basement.

4. The parties agree to keep the terms of this settlement, and the allegations giving rise to this Agreement, completely confidential, and will not hereinafter disclose any information concerning them to anyone.

5. This Agreement shall be binding upon, and inure to the benefit of, each of the parties to this Agreement, and upon their respective heirs, administrators, representatives, executors and successors, if any.

6. This Agreement constitutes the entire agreement between the parties hereto and supersedes any and all other agreements, understand-

ings, negotiations, or discussions, either oral or in writing, express or implied between the parties hereto.

7. This Agreement may not be amended, altered, modified or otherwise changed, except in a writing executed by the parties hereto.

IN WITNESS WHEREOF, the parties hereto have caused this agreement to be executed as of the date above set forth.

BY:_____

JOHN SMITH

BY:_____

JANE DOE

VERIFICATION

STATE OF _____)

COUNTY OF _____)

On the _____ day of _____, _____, before me personally came JOHN SMITH and JANE DOE, to me known to be the individuals described in and who executed the foregoing instrument, and acknowledged that they executed the same.

_____

NOTARY PUBLIC

APPENDIX 16:
MONETARY LIMITS IN SMALL CLAIMS
COURT BY STATE

STATE	MONETARY LIMIT
Alabama	$3000
Alaska	$7500
Arizona	$2500
Arkansas	$5000
California	$5000
Colorado	$7500
Connecticut	$3500
Delaware	$15000
District of Columbia	$5000
Florida	$5000
Georgia	$15000
Hawaii	$3500
Idaho	$4000
Illinois	$5000
Indiana	$3000
Iowa	$5000
Kansas	$4000
Kentucky	$1500
Louisiana	$3000
Maine	$4500
Maryland	$5000
Massachusetts	$2000
Michigan	$3000
Minnesota	$7500

STATE	MONETARY LIMIT
Mississippi	$2500
Missouri	$3000
Montana	$3000
Nebraska	$2400
Nevada	$5000
New Hampshire	$5000
New Jersey	$3000
New Mexico	$10000
New York	$3000
North Carolina	$4000
North Dakota	$5000
Ohio	$3000
Oklahoma	$4500
Oregon	$5000
Pennsylvania	$10000
Rhode Island	$1500
South Carolina	$7500
South Dakota	$8000
Tennessee	$10000
Texas	$5000
Utah	$7500
Vermont	$3500
Virginia	$2000
Washington	$4000
West Virginia	$5000
Wisconsin	$5000
Wyoming	$7000

APPENDIX 17:
STATE SMALL CLAIMS COURT ONLINE
INFORMATION WEBSITES

STATE	COURT WEBSITE
Alabama	http://www.alacourt.gov/Forms/SmallClaims
Alaska	http://www.state.ak.us/courts/ctinfo.htm
Arizona	http://www.supreme.state.az.us/info/brochures/smclaims.htm
Arkansas	http://www.arkbar.com/publications/publication_public.html#Small
California	http://www.courtinfo.ca.gov/selfhelp/smallclaims
Colorado	http://www.ago.state.co.us/consprot/smclaim.htm/smallclaims.html
Connecticut	http://www.jud.state.ct.us/faq/smallclaims.html
Delaware	http://courts.state.de.us/How%20To/court%20proceedings/?JPCourt.htm
District of Columbia	http://www.dccourts.gov/dccourts/superior/civil/small_claims_faq.jsp
Florida	http://www.miami-dadeclerk.com/dadecoc
Georgia	http://www2.state.ga.us/GaOCA/magistra1.htm
Hawaii	http://www.state.hi.us/dcca/ocp/smallclaim.html
Idaho	http://www2.state.id.us/fourthjudicial/HOME%20PAGE.htm
Illinois	http://circuit-court.co.monroe.il.us/small_claims.htm
Indiana	http://www.small-claims-court.com
Iowa	http://www.judicial.state.ia.us/about/descript/district.asp
Kansas	http://www.kscourts.org/dstcts/4claims.htm
Kentucky	http://www.kycourts.net
Louisiana	http://brgov.com/dept/citycourt/civilfaqs.htm
Maine	http://www.courts.state.me.us/mainecourts/smallclaims/smallclaimsguide/index.html
Maryland	http://www.courts.state.md.us/district/brochures/dccv01br.html
Massachusetts	http://www.mass.gov/courts/courtsandjudges/courts/districtcourt/municipalitiesbydistct.html
Michigan	http://courts.michigan.gov/scao/faqs/QandA_civil.htm#small

STATE	COURT WEBSITE
Minnesota	http://www.co.stearns.mn.us/departments/other/court/conccourt.htm
Mississippi	http://www.mississippi.gov/frameset.jsp?URL=http://www.mssc.state.ms.us/
Missouri	http://www.mobar.org/pamphlet/smllclam.htm
Montana	http://www.lawlibrary.state.mt.us/dscgi/ds.py/View/Collection-2930
Nebraska	http://court.nol.org/publications/smallclaims.htm
Nevada	http://www.co.clark.nv.us/justicecourt_lv/smallclaim.htm
New Hampshire	http://doj.nh.gov/consumer/scc.html
New Jersey	http://www.judiciary.state.nj.us/civil/civ-02.htm
New Mexico	http://www.ago.state.nm.us/divs/cons/cons_acc_court.htm
New York	http://www.consumer.state.ny.us/clahm/Clahm-Small_Claims_Court.htm
North Carolina	http://www.legalaidnc.org/publications/SmallClaimsCourt/SmClaims-FRAME.htm
North Dakota	http://www.court.state.nd.us/COURT/courts.htm
Ohio	http://www.ag.state.oh.us/online%5Fpublications/consumer%5Fprotection/smclaims.htm
Oklahoma	http://www.oklahomacounty.org/courtclerk/SmallClaimsProcedures.htm
Oregon	http://www.ojd.state.or.us/mar/smallclaims.htm
Pennsylvania	http://courts.phila.gov/municipal
Rhode Island	http://www.courts.state.ri.us/district/smallclaims.htm
South Carolina	http://www3.charlestoncounty.org/docs/Magistrates/summfaq.htm#MagCivil2
South Dakota	http://www.sdjudicial.com
Tennessee	http://www.tba.org/lawbytes/T9_1800.html
Texas	http://williamson-county.org/JP/faq.html
Utah	http://www.utcourts.gov/howto/smallclaims
Vermont	http://www.vermontjudiciary.org/courts/superior/smclaims.htm
Virginia	http://www.courts.state.va.us/pamphlets/small_claims.html
Washington	http://www.courts.wa.gov/newsinfo/resources/?fa=newsinfo_jury.scc&altMenu=smal
West Virginia	http://www.state.wv.us/wvsca/wvsystem.htm#magistrate
Wisconsin	http://www.wicourts.gov/about/pubs/circuit/smallclaimsguide.htm
Wyoming	http://courts.state.wy.us/wyoming_court_rules.htm

APPENDIX 18:
NOTICE, CLAIM AND SUMMONS TO
APPEAR FOR TRIAL

Small Claims Court _____ County, Colorado
Court Address:

PLAINTIFF(S): _____
Address: _____
City/State/Zip: _____
Phone: Home _____ Work _____ Cell _____

v.
DEFENDANT(1): _____
Address: _____
City/State/Zip: _____
Phone: Home _____ Work _____ Cell _____
DEFENDANT(2): _____
Address: _____
City/State/Zip: _____
Phone: Home _____ Work _____ Cell _____

▲ **COURT USE ONLY** ▲
Case Number:

S

Division   Courtroom

NOTICE, CLAIM AND SUMMONS TO APPEAR FOR TRIAL (Part 1)

If Defendant(s) is/are other than a person, call the Secretary of State's office at (303) 894-2200, or go on-line at www.sos.state.co.us to determine the registered agent for service of this notice. Please enter name and address of the agent. Name: _____ Address: _____

The Defendant(s) is/are in the military service: ❑ Yes ❑ No ❑ Unknown   I am an attorney: ❑ Yes ❑ No
The Defendant(s) reside(s), is/are regularly employed, has/have an office for the transaction of business, or is/are a student in this county, or the Defendant(s) own(s) the rental property in the county that is the subject of this claim.
❑ Yes ❑ No
I/We understand that it is my/our responsibility to have the Defendant(s) served by a disinterested person over the age of 18 no later than 15 days prior to the trial and to provide the Court with written proof of service. ❑ Yes ❑ No

NOTICE AND SUMMONS TO APPEAR FOR TRIAL

To the Defendant(s):
You are scheduled to have your trial in this case on (date) _____ (time) _____ at the Court address stated in the above caption. Bring with you all books, papers and witnesses you need to establish your defense. IF YOU DO NOT APPEAR, JUDGMENT WILL BE ENTERED AGAINST YOU. If you wish to defend the claim or present a counterclaim, you must provide a written response or written counterclaim on or before the scheduled trial date and pay a **NONREFUNDABLE** filing fee.

Dated: _____   _____
                                 Clerk of Court/Deputy Clerk

PLAINTIFF(S) S CLAIM
The Defendant(s) owe(s) me $ _____, which includes penalties, plus interest and costs allowed by law, and/or should be ordered to return property, perform a contract or set aside a contract or comply with a restrictive covenant for the following reasons. (If seeking return of property, please describe the property being requested).
_____
_____
_____
_____
_____
_____

Note: The combined value of money property specific performance or cost to remedy a covenant violation cannot exceed $7 500.00.

I/We declare under penalty of perjury that the above statements are true and correct, and that I/we have not filed more than two claims in any one or more small claims courts in Colorado during this month, nor more than 18 claims in this calendar year.

Dated: _____   _____
                                 Plaintiff's Signature
                                 _____
                                 Plaintiff's Signature

JDF 250 R7/04 (PART 1/ PAGE 1)   NOTICE, CLAIM AND SUMMONS TO APPEAR FOR TRIAL   COURT COPY

Small Claims Court _____ County, Colorado
Court Address:

PLAINTIFF(S): _____
Address: _____
City/State/Zip: _____
Phone: Home _____ Work _____ Cell _____

v.
DEFENDANT(1): _____
Address: _____
City/State/Zip: _____
Phone: Home _____ Work _____ Cell _____
DEFENDANT(2): _____
Address: _____
City/State/Zip: _____
Phone: Home _____ Work _____ Cell _____

▲ COURT USE ONLY ▲
Case Number:

S

Division   Courtroom

NOTICE CLAIM AND SUMMONS TO APPEAR FOR TRIAL (Part 2)

If Defendant(s) is/are other than a person, call the Secretary of State's office at (303) 894-2200, or go on-line at www.sos.state.co.us to determine the registered agent for service of this notice. Please enter name and address of the agent. Name: _____ Address: _____

The Defendant(s) is/are in the military service: ❑ Yes ❑ No ❑ Unknown   I am an attorney: ❑ Yes ❑ No
The Defendant(s) reside(s), is/are regularly employed, has/have an office for the transaction of business, or is/are a student in this county, or the Defendant(s) own(s) the rental property in the county that is the subject of this claim.
❑ Yes ❑ No
I/We understand that it is my/our responsibility to have the Defendant(s) served by a disinterested person over the age of 18 no later than 15 days prior to the trial and to provide the Court with written proof of service. ❑ Yes ❑ No

NOTICE AND SUMMONS TO APPEAR FOR TRIAL

To the Defendant(s):
You are scheduled to have your trial in this case on (date) _____ (time) _____ at the Court address stated in the above caption. Bring with you all books, papers and witnesses you need to establish your defense. **IF YOU DO NOT APPEAR JUDGMENT WILL BE ENTERED AGAINST YOU.** If you wish to defend the claim or present a counterclaim, you must provide a written response or written counterclaim on or before the scheduled trial date and pay a **NONREFUNDABLE** filing fee.

Dated: _____

_____
Clerk of Court/Deputy Clerk

PLAINTIFF(S) S CLAIM
The Defendant(s) owe(s) me $_____, which includes penalties, plus interest and costs allowed by law, and/or should be ordered to return property, perform a contract or set aside a contract or comply with a restrictive covenant for the following reasons. (If seeking return of property, please describe the property being requested).

_____
_____
_____
_____

Note: The combined value of money property specific performance or cost to remedy a covenant violation cannot exceed $7 500.00.

I/We declare under penalty of perjury that the above statements are true and correct, and that I/we have not filed more than two claims in any one or more small claims courts in Colorado during this month, nor more than 18 claims in this calendar year.

Dated: _____

_____
Plaintiff's Signature

_____
Plaintiff's Signature

You must complete and fill out a response and or counterclaim on reverse side of Defendant s copy and bring to Court.
JDF 250   R7/04 (PART 2/ PAGE 2)   NOTICE, CLAIM AND SUMMONS TO APPEAR FOR TRIAL   DEFENDANT'S COPY

DEFENDANT S RESPONSE (Fee for responding is as stated in A below). I do not owe the Plaintiff(s) or am not responsible to the Plaintiff(s) because:

_____

_____

DEFENDANT S COUNTERCLAIM (If responding or submitting a counterclaim, pay the appropriate filing fees).
The Plaintiff(s) owe(s) me $_____, which includes penalties, plus interest and costs allowed by law and/or should be ordered to return property, perform a contract or set aside a contract or comply with a restrictive covenant for the following reasons. (If seeking return of property, please describe the property being requested).

_____

_____

- ❑   The amount of my/our counterclaim does not exceed the jurisdictional amount of the Small Claims Court of $7,500.00.
- ❑   The amount of my/our counterclaim exceeds the jurisdictional amount of the Small Claims Court, but I/we wish to limit the amount that I/we wish to recover from the Plaintiff to $7,500.00.
- ❑   The amount of my/our counterclaim exceeds the jurisdictional amount of the Small Claims Court, and I/we wish to have the case sent to ❑County Court (only if I/we wish to limit the amount I/we can recover from the plaintiff to $15,000.00) ❑District Court (I /we do not wish to limit the amount I/we can recover from the Plaintiff(s)) and will pay the appropriate filing fee. I/we am/are filing a Notice of Removal and paying the appropriate filing fee to the Court at this time.

I am an attorney.   ❑Yes ❑No
I declare under penalty of perjury that this information is true and correct.
I certify that I mailed a copy of the answer/counterclaim to the Plaintiff(s) at the address(es) stated on this form on _____ (date).

_____
Defendant's Address

Defendant's Signature	Date	Telephone #: Home	Work	Cell

INFORMATION FOR DEFENDANTS IN SMALL CLAIMS CASES

A.   **FILING FEES.**
Response without a counterclaim:
- ♦   **Claim $500.00 or less: $10.00**   Claim over $500.00 but less than $7,500.00: $25.00

Response with a counterclaim:
- ♦   If Plaintiff,s claim is less than $500.00 and counterclaim is less than $500.00: $15.00
- ♦   If Plaintiff,s claim is less than $500.00 and counterclaim is between $500.01 - $7,500.00: $30.00
- ♦   If Plaintiff s claim is between $500.01 and $7,500.00 and counterclaim is between $.01 and $7,500.00: $30.00

B.   **RESPONSE.** You have been served with a Summons. If you fail to appear on the trial date shown on this notice, judgment may be entered against you. If you wish to defend the claim or present a counterclaim, you must **file with the Court Clerk a written response or counterclaim** on or before the scheduled trial date, provide a copy to the Plaintiff(s), pay the appropriate **nonrefundable** filing fee, and appear on the date set for trial in this notice with all evidence and witnesses needed to establish your defense.

C.   **SUBPOENAS.** Upon your request, the clerk will issue a subpoena to require witnesses to appear or bring documents for your trial. It is your responsibility to complete the information needed on the subpoena and to have the subpoena served. Subpoenas must be served personally and may be served by a person over the age of 18 that is not a party to the case. Subpoenas must be accompanied by a check for payment of witness fees and mileage for any witnesses served.

D.   **COUNTERCLAIM.** If you have a claim against the Plaintiff(s), you must **FILE WITH THE COURT CLERK** the Defendant's counterclaim at the top of this form, provide a copy of the counterclaim to the Plaintiff(s) prior to the trial, and pay the appropriate **nonrefundable** filing fee. If you settle your counterclaim before trial, notify the Small Claims Court and the Plaintiff(s) in writing. **If you want your case heard by a Court of greater jurisdiction, you must complete and file this form, pay the appropriate filing fee (County = $46.00, District = $136.00) and file a Notice of Removal (JDF 251) at least seven days before the trial date shown on this Notice.**

E.   **TRIAL RESPONSIBILITY.** You have a right to a trial. Bring all evidence necessary to establish your defense and/or counterclaim: books, papers, repair bills, photographs or other exhibits. If the suit involves the delivery of personal property, be prepared to deliver the property immediately after trial. Be on time. If you are late, the Court may enter judgment against you.

F.   **APPEAL.** If you wish to appeal, you must file your appeal within 15 days of the judgment and proceed according to C.R.C.P 411.

G.   **JUDGMENT. THE COURT DOES NOT COLLECT ANY JUDGMENT,** but will help with the necessary forms.
Money Judgment. If judgment is entered against you, you are expected to immediately pay the judgment, including filing fees and court costs. If the judgment is not paid immediately, you must answer questions about your assets and income and the other party can obtain a writ of garnishment or execution against your wages or property. Once the judgment is paid, you are entitled to have the judgment satisfied.
Non-monetary Judgment. If the Court orders immediate possession of the property, performance of a contract, setting aside of a contract or compliance with a restrictive covenant, your failure to comply with the Court order may result in an award of damages and/or being held in contempt.

H.   **CASE INQUIRIES.** When inquiring about this case, refer to the case number on this notice. Direct all inquiries to the clerk, not the judge or magistrate.

I.   **ATTORNEY.** If you want to be represented by an attorney, you or your attorney must file a Notice of Representation of Attorney (JDF 256) at least seven days before the trial date on this notice. Then the Plaintiff(s) may have representation by an attorney. If the Plaintiff(s) is/are an attorney, you also may be represented by an attorney without filing a notice of representation. Even if there are attorneys in the case, the rules and procedures of the Small Claims Court will still apply.

J.   **JUDICIAL OFFICER.** A magistrate or a judge may hear your case. If you want a judge to hear your case, you must file an Objection to a Magistrate Hearing Case (JDF 259) at least seven days before the trial date set in this notice. The rules and procedures of the Small Claims Court will still apply.

JDF 250   R7/04 (PART 2/ PAGE 3)   NOTICE, CLAIM AND SUMMONS TO APPEAR FOR TRIAL   DEFENDANT'S COPY

Small Claims Court _____ County, Colorado
Court Address:

_____

PLAINTIFF(S): _____
Address: _____
City/State/Zip: _____
Phone: Home _____ Work _____ Cell _____

v.
DEFENDANT(1): _____
Address: _____
City/State/Zip: _____
Phone: Home _____ Work _____ Cell _____
DEFENDANT(2): _____
Address: _____
City/State/Zip: _____
Phone: Home _____ Work _____ Cell _____

▲   COURT USE ONLY   ▲
Case Number:

S

Division   Courtroom

NOTICE CLAIM AND SUMMONS TO APPEAR FOR TRIAL (Part 3)

If Defendant(s) is/are other than a person, call the Secretary of State's office at (303) 894-2200, or go on-line at www.sos.state.co.us to determine the registered agent for service of this notice. Please enter name and address of the agent. Name: _____ Address: _____

The Defendant(s) is/are in the military service: ❑ Yes ❑ No ❑ Unknown   I am an attorney: ❑ Yes ❑ No
The Defendant(s) reside(s), is/are regularly employed, has/have an office for the transaction of business, or is/are a student in this county, or the Defendant(s) own(s) the rental property in the county that is the subject of this claim.
❑ Yes ❑ No
I/We understand that it is my/our responsibility to have the Defendant(s) served by a disinterested person over the age of 18 no later than 15 days prior to the trial and to provide the Court with written proof of service. ❑ Yes ❑ No

NOTICE AND SUMMONS TO APPEAR FOR TRIAL
To the Defendant(s):
You are scheduled to have your trial in this case on (date) _____ (time) _____ at the Court address stated in the above caption. Bring with you all books, papers and witnesses you need to establish your defense. **IF YOU DO NOT APPEAR JUDGMENT WILL BE ENTERED AGAINST YOU.** If you wish to defend the claim or present a counterclaim, you must provide a written response or written counterclaim on or before the scheduled trial date and pay a **NONREFUNDABLE** filing fee.

Dated: _____   _____
                                        Clerk of Court/Deputy Clerk

PLAINTIFF(S) S CLAIM
The Defendant(s) owe(s) me $_____, which includes penalties, plus interest and costs allowed by law, and/or should be ordered to return property, perform a contract or set aside a contract or comply with a restrictive covenant for the following reasons. (If seeking return of property, please describe the property being requested).

_____
_____
_____
_____
_____
_____

Note: The combined value of money property specific performance or cost to remedy a covenant violation cannot exceed $7 500.00.

I/We declare under penalty of perjury that the above statements are true and correct, and that I/we have not filed more than two claims in any one or more small claims courts in Colorado during this month, nor more than 18 claims in this calendar year.

Dated: _____   _____
                                                      Plaintiff's Signature

                                                      _____
                                                      Plaintiff's Signature

JDF 250   R7/04 (PART 3/ PAGE 4)   NOTICE, CLAIM AND SUMMONS TO APPEAR FOR TRIAL   PLAINTIFF'S COPY

INFORMATION FOR PLAINTIFFS IN SMALL CLAIMS CASES

A. **FILING.** You may file your claim in this Court if:
1. Your claim is for money, property, specific performance or rescission of a contract, or enforcement of a restrictive covenant that does not exceed $7,500.00. You may reduce a larger claim and waive the balance. You cannot divide a claim and file two separate cases.
2. At least one of the parties you sue resides, is regularly employed, has an office for the transaction of business, or is a student in this county, or they own rental property in the county that is the subject of this claim.
3. You pay the clerk one of the following **NONREFUNDABLE** filing fees.
   - **Claim $500.00 or less:** $15.00
   - **Claim over $500.00 but less than $7 500.00:** $39.00

B. **SERVICE.** This notice to appear must be served at least 15 days prior to the trial. It may be served by:
1. Any person over 18 years of age who is not a party to this action.
2. Sheriff or process server.
3. Certified Mail that is mailed by the clerk. You must deposit the cost for certified mail in advance.

C. **SETTLEMENT.** If you settle your claim before trial, you must notify the Small Claims Court and Defendant in writing.

D. **SUBPOENAS.** Upon your request, the clerk will issue a subpoena to require witnesses to appear or bring documents for your trial. It is your responsibility to complete the information needed on the subpoena and to have the subpoena served. Subpoenas must be served personally and may be served by a person over the age of 18 that is not a party to the case. Subpoenas must be accompanied by a check for payment of witness fees and mileage for any witnesses served.

E. **TRIAL RESPONSIBILITY.** You have a right to a trial. Bring all evidence necessary to prove your case: books, papers, repair bills, photographs or other exhibits. Be on time. If you are late or do not appear, the Court may enter judgment in favor of the Defendant and against you if the Defendant filed a counterclaim.

F. **APPEAL.** If you wish to appeal, you must file your appeal within 15 days of the judgment and proceed according to C.R.C.P. 411.

G. **JUDGMENT. THE COURT DOES NOT COLLECT ANY JUDGMENT,** but will help with the necessary forms.
Money Judgment. If judgment is entered in favor of the Defendant and against you, you are expected to immediately pay the judgment, including filing fees and court costs. If the judgment is not paid immediately, you must answer questions about your assets and income and the other party can obtain a writ of garnishment or execution against your wages or property. Once the judgment is paid, you are entitled to have the judgment satisfied.
Non-monetary Judgment. If the Court orders immediate possession of the property, performance of a contract, setting aside of a contract or compliance with a restrictive covenant, failure to comply with the Court order may result in an award of damages and or being held in contempt.

H. **CASE INQUIRIES.** When inquiring about this case, refer to the case number on the other side of this document. Direct all inquiries to the clerk, not the judge or magistrate.

I. **ATTORNEY.** If the Defendant(s) want(s) to be represented by an attorney, the Defendant(s) or attorney must file a Notice of Representation of Attorney (JDF 256) at least seven days before the trial date on this notice. Then, you may have representation by an attorney. If either party is an attorney, the other party may be represented by an attorney without filing a notice of representation. Even if there are attorneys in the case, the rules and procedures of the Small Claims Court will still apply.

J. **JUDICIAL OFFICER.** A magistrate or judge may hear your case. If you want a judge to hear your case, you must file an Objection to a Magistrate Hearing Case (JDF 259) at least seven days before the trial date set in this notice. The rules and procedures of the Small Claims Court will still apply.

NOTICE, CLAIM AND SUMMONS TO APPEAR FOR TRIAL

Small Claims Court _____ County, Colorado Court Address:	
PLAINTIFF(S): _____ Address: _____ City/State/Zip: _____ Phone: Home _____ Work _____ Cell _____ v. **DEFENDANT(1):** _____ Address: _____ City/State/Zip: _____ Phone: Home _____ Work _____ Cell _____ **DEFENDANT(2):** _____ Address: _____ City/State/Zip: _____ Phone: Home _____ Work _____ Cell _____	▲ **COURT USE ONLY** ▲ Case Number: **S** Division Courtroom

NOTICE CLAIM AND SUMMONS TO APPEAR FOR TRIAL (Part 4)

If Defendant(s) is/are other than a person, call the Secretary of State's office at (303) 894-2200, or go on-line at www.sos.state.co.us to determine the registered agent for service of this notice. Please enter name and address of the agent. Name: _____ Address: _____

The Defendant(s) is/are in the military service: ❑ Yes ❑ No ❑ Unknown   I am an attorney: ❑ Yes ❑ No
The Defendant(s) reside(s), is/are regularly employed, has/have an office for the transaction of business, or is/are a student in this county, or the Defendant(s) own(s) the rental property in the county that is the subject of this claim.
❑ Yes ❑ No
I/We understand that it is my/our responsibility to have the Defendant(s) served by a disinterested person over the age of 18 no later than 15 days prior to the trial and to provide the Court with written proof of service. ❑ Yes ❑ No

NOTICE AND SUMMONS TO APPEAR FOR TRIAL

To the Defendant(s):
You are scheduled to have your trial in this case on (date) _____ (time) _____ at the Court address stated in the above caption. Bring with you all books, papers and witnesses you need to establish your defense. **IF YOU DO NOT APPEAR JUDGMENT WILL BE ENTERED AGAINST YOU.** If you wish to defend the claim or present a counterclaim, you must provide a written response or written counterclaim on ore before the scheduled trial date and pay a **NONREFUNDABLE** filing fee.

Dated: _____   _____
                                                 Clerk of Court/Deputy Clerk

PLAINTIFF(S) S CLAIM
The Defendant(s) owe(s) me $_____, which includes penalties, plus interest and costs allowed by law, and/or should be ordered to return property, perform a contract or set aside a contract or comply with a restrictive covenant for the following reasons. (If seeking return of property, please describe the property being requested).

_____
_____
_____
_____
_____

Note: The combined value of money property specific performance or cost to remedy a covenant violation cannot exceed $7 500.00

I/We declare under penalty of perjury that the above statements are true and correct, and that I/we have not filed more than two claims in any one or more small claims courts in Colorado during this month, nor more than 18 claims in this calendar year.

Dated: _____   _____
                                                   Plaintiff's Signature

                                                   Plaintiff's Signature

JDF 250   R7/04 (PART 4/ PAGE 6)   NOTICE, CLAIM AND SUMMONS TO APPEAR FOR TRIAL   COURT COPY

Case Name _____ v. _____   Case Number: _____

AFFIDAVIT OF SERVICE
(Must be returned to Court)

I personally hand delivered a copy of the foregoing Notice, Claim and Summons to Appear for Trial, on the following:

Name of Person Served   **Date of Service**   **Address of Service**
                                                                                    (Street County City State)

If the person on whom service was made is not the named party to be served, I served the Notice, Claim and Summons to Appear for Trial:

❑   At the regular place of abode of the person to be served, by leaving the Notice with a person over the age of 18 years who regularly resides at the place of abode. (Identify relationship to defendant _____.)

❑   At the regular place of business of the person to be served, by leaving the Notice with that person's secretary, bookkeeper, chief clerk, office receptionist/assistant or partner. (Circle title of person who was served.)

❑   By leaving the Notice with a partner, limited partner, associate, manager, elected official, receptionist/assistant, bookkeeper or general agent of the partnership, limited liability company, or other non-corporate entity, which was to be served. (Circle title of person who was served.)

❑   By leaving the Notice with an officer, manager, receptionist/assistant, legal assistant, paid legal advisor or general agent, registered agent for service of process, stockholder or principal employee of the corporation, that was to be served. (Circle title of person who was served.)

I am over the age of 18 years, and I am not an interested party in this matter.

I have charged the following fees for my services in this matter:

❑ Private process server
❑ Sheriff, _____County
   Fee $ _____   Mileage $ _____

_____
Signature of Process Server

_____
Name (Print or type)

Subscribed and affirmed, or sworn to before me in the County of _____, State of _____, this _____ day of _____, 20 _____.

My commission expires: _____

_____
Notary Public

CERTIFICATE OF SERVICE BY MAILING
(To be performed by Clerk within three days of filing)

I hereby certify that on (date)_____, I mailed a true and correct copy of the NOTICE, CLAIM, AND SUMMONS TO APPEAR FOR TRIAL, by placing it in the United States Mail, postage pre-paid to the Defendant(s) at the address(es) listed above.

_____
Clerk of Court/Deputy Clerk

❑ (If applicable) Plaintiff(s) notified of non-service on (date)_____. Clerk's Initials _____

JDF 250 R7/04 (PART 4/ PAGE 7)   NOTICE, CLAIM AND SUMMONS TO APPEAR FOR TRIAL   COURT COPY

APPENDIX 19:
STATEMENT OF CLAIM

STATE OF MAINE

DISTRICT COURT
Location _____
Docket No. _____

_____Plaintiff

_____

_____

    v.   **STATEMENT OF CLAIM**
                                 (Small Claims)

_____Defendant

_____

_____

Briefly describe your claim, including relevant dates:
_____
_____
_____
_____
_____

The plaintiff requests a judgment against the defendant in the amount of $_____
plus costs. *If you are asking for an order to repair or return property, or to refund money, or to reform or rescind an agreement, state your request:*
_____
_____
_____

Date: _____   _____
                                        Signature

Attorney for Plaintiff: _____
Address:_____
_____
Telephone:_____

****

IMPORTANT NOTICE TO PARTIES

To the plaintiff and the defendant:
    You will be notified of the hearing date and time of this case by the clerk of the court. The notice of hearing will be sent to you by regular mail at the address given above unless you notify the clerk of a different address. If the above address is incorrect or if your address changes, you must promptly notify the clerk in writing. Your failure to notify the clerk of an address change will mean that you may not receive notice of the hearing.

IF THE PLAINTIFF FAILS TO APPEAR AT THE HEARING, THE CASE WILL BE DISMISSED. IF THE DEFENDANT FAILS TO APPEAR, A DEFAULT JUDGMENT MAY BE ENTERED AGAINST THE DEFENDANT FOR THE RELIEF SOUGHT BY THE PLAINTIFF.

The address of the court is:

STATE OF MAINE

_____ County

I have this day made service of the Statement of Claim upon the defendant _____

_____

☐   by delivering a copy of the Statement to the defendant in hand at _____

_____

☐   by leaving a copy of the Statement with _____, a

person of suitable age and discretion at the defendant's dwelling house or usual place of abode

located at _____

Date: _____   _____
                                     Deputy Sheriff

Service:

        Travel $_____
        Postage $_____

        Total $_____

APPENDIX 20:
SMALL CLAIMS WRIT AND NOTICE OF SUIT

SMALL CLAIMS WRIT AND NOTICE OF SUIT	CONNECTICUT SUPERIOR COURT SMALL CLAIMS SESSION	DOCKET NO. SC
JD-CV-40 Rev. 4-01 C.G.S. § 51-15 Pr. Bk. § 24-1 et seq.	Type or print legibly. Complete original and make one copy for each party to the action. File the original and all copies with the clerk. Also, include one "Instructions to Defendant" for each defendant and submit the appropriate entry fee.	ANSWER DATE

SMALL CLAIMS AREA LOCATION
☐ G.A. _____ ☐ HOUSING SESSION AT: _____ ☐ JUDICIAL DISTRICT AT: _____

P L T F # 1	NAME ADDRESS AND ZIP CODE OF PLAINTIFF #1			P L T F # 2	NAME ADDRESS AND ZIP CODE OF PLAINTIFF #2		
	TELEPHONE NO. (w/area code)	("X" ONE) ☐ LLC ☐ PARTNERSHIP ☐ INDIVIDUAL ☐ CORPORATION			TELEPHONE NO. (w/area code)	("X" ONE) ☐ LLC ☐ PARTNERSHIP ☐ INDIVIDUAL ☐ CORPORATION	

ATTORNEY FOR PLAINTIFF(S)		JURIS NO.	TELEPHONE NO. (w/area code)

D E F # 1	NAME ADDRESS AND ZIP CODE OF DEFENDANT #1			D E F # 2	NAME ADDRESS AND ZIP CODE OF DEFENDANT #2		
	TELEPHONE NO. (w/area code)	("X" ONE) ☐ LLC ☐ PARTNERSHIP ☐ INDIVIDUAL ☐ CORPORATION			TELEPHONE NO. (w/area code)	("X" ONE) ☐ LLC ☐ PARTNERSHIP ☐ INDIVIDUAL ☐ CORPORATION	

FOR COURT USE ONLY:	ATTORNEY FOR DEFENDANT(S)		JURIS NO.	TELEPHONE NO. (w/area code)

YOU ARE BEING SUED.
THE ABOVE PLAINTIFF(S) **CLAIMS YOU OWE**
PLUS COURT COSTS, FOR THE FOLLOWING REASONS:

AMOUNT DUE	TOWN WHERE TRANSACTION/INJURY OCCURRED OR PREMISES LOCATED

The undersigned, being duly sworn, deposes and says that the signer has read the claim and, to the best of the signer's knowledge, information and belief, there is good ground to support it.

SIGNED X	TYPE IN NAME AND TITLE OF PERSON SIGNING AT LEFT
SUBSCRIBED AND SWORN TO BEFORE ME ON (Date)	SIGNED (Clerk, Notary, Comm. of Sup. Ct.) X

The undersigned deposes and says: **MILITARY SERVICE AFFIDAVIT**

☐ that the undersigned is unable to determine whether or not the defendant(s) in this action are in the military or naval service of the United States.

☐ that the defendant is in the military or naval service of the United States.

☐ that no defendant in this action is in the military or naval service of the United States, and that, to the personal knowledge of the undersigned *(state facts showing defendant is not in such service)*

FOR COURT USE ONLY
DATE ENTERED

SIGNATURE AND TITLE **X**

SUBSCRIBED AND SWORN TO BEFORE ME ON (Date)	SIGNED (Clerk, Notary, Comm. of Sup. Ct.) X
SIGNED (Clerk) X	

DISTRIBUTION: ORIGINAL - Court   COPY 1- Defendant   COPY 2 - Defendant   COPY 3 - Plaintiff   *www.jud.state.ct.us*

SMALL CLAIMS WRIT AND NOTICE OF SUIT	CONNECTICUT SUPERIOR COURT SMALL CLAIMS SESSION	DOCKET NO. SC
JD-CV-40 Rev. 4-01 C.G.S. § 51-15 Pr. Bk. § 24-1 et seq.	Type or print legibly. Complete original and make one copy for each party to the action. File the original and all copies with the clerk. Also, include one "Instructions to Defendant" for each defendant and submit the appropriate entry fee.	ANSWER DATE

SMALL CLAIMS AREA LOCATION

☐ G.A. _____ ☐ HOUSING SESSION AT: _____   ☐ JUDICIAL DISTRICT AT: _____

P L T F #1
NAME ADDRESS AND ZIP CODE OF PLAINTIFF #1

TELEPHONE NO. (w/area code) ("X" ONE) ☐ LLC ☐ PARTNERSHIP ☐ INDIVIDUAL ☐ CORPORATION

P L T F #2
NAME ADDRESS AND ZIP CODE OF PLAINTIFF #2

TELEPHONE NO. (w/area code) ("X" ONE) ☐ LLC ☐ PARTNERSHIP ☐ INDIVIDUAL ☐ CORPORATION

ATTORNEY FOR PLAINTIFF(S)   JURIS NO.   TELEPHONE NO. (w/area code)

D E F #1
NAME ADDRESS AND ZIP CODE OF DEFENDANT #1

TELEPHONE NO. (w/area code) ("X" ONE) ☐ LLC ☐ PARTNERSHIP ☐ INDIVIDUAL ☐ CORPORATION

D E F #2
NAME ADDRESS AND ZIP CODE OF DEFENDANT #2

TELEPHONE NO. (w/area code) ("X" ONE) ☐ LLC ☐ PARTNERSHIP ☐ INDIVIDUAL ☐ CORPORATION

FOR COURT USE ONLY: ATTORNEY FOR DEFENDANT(S)   JURIS NO.   TELEPHONE NO. (w/area code)

YOU ARE BEING SUED.
THE ABOVE PLAINTIFF(S) **CLAIMS YOU OWE**
PLUS COURT COSTS, FOR THE FOLLOWING REASONS:

AMOUNT DUE

TOWN WHERE TRANSACTION/INJURY OCCURRED OR PREMISES LOCATED

The undersigned, being duly sworn, deposes and says that the signer has read the claim and, to the best of the signer's knowledge, information and belief, there is good ground to support it.

SIGNED X	TYPE IN NAME AND TITLE OF PERSON SIGNING AT LEFT
SUBSCRIBED AND SWORN TO BEFORE ME ON (Date)	SIGNED (Clerk, Notary, Comm. of Sup. Ct.) X

The undersigned deposes and says: **MILITARY SERVICE AFFIDAVIT**

☐ that the undersigned is unable to determine whether or not the defendant(s) in this action are in the military or naval service of the United States.

☐ that the defendant is in the military or naval service of the United States.

☐ that no defendant in this action is in the military or naval service of the United States, and that, to the personal knowledge of the undersigned (state facts showing defendant is not in such service)

FOR COURT USE ONLY
DATE ENTERED

DOCKET NO.

SIGNATURE AND TITLE X _____

SUBSCRIBED AND SWORN TO BEFORE ME ON (Date)	SIGNED (Clerk, Notary, Comm. of Sup. Ct.) X
SIGNED (Clerk) X	

DISTRIBUTION: ORIGINAL - Court   COPY 1- Defendant   COPY 2 - Defendant   COPY 3 - Plaintiff   *www.jud.state.ct.us*

SMALL CLAIMS WRIT AND NOTICE OF SUIT

JD-CV-40 Rev. 4-01
C.G.S. § 51-15
Pr. Bk. § 24-1 et seq.

CONNECTICUT SUPERIOR COURT SMALL CLAIMS SESSION

Type or print legibly. Complete original and make one copy for each party to the action. File the original and all copies with the clerk. Also, include one "Instructions to Defendant" for each defendant and submit the appropriate entry fee.

DOCKET NO.
SC

ANSWER DATE

SMALL CLAIMS AREA LOCATION

☐ G.A. _____ ☐ HOUSING SESSION AT: _____ ☐ JUDICIAL DISTRICT AT: _____

P L T F # 1	NAME ADDRESS AND ZIP CODE OF PLAINTIFF #1	P L T F # 2	NAME ADDRESS AND ZIP CODE OF PLAINTIFF #2
	TELEPHONE NO. (w/area code) ("X" ONE) ☐ LLC ☐ PARTNERSHIP ☐ INDIVIDUAL ☐ CORPORATION		TELEPHONE NO. (w/area code) ("X" ONE) ☐ LLC ☐ PARTNERSHIP ☐ INDIVIDUAL ☐ CORPORATION

ATTORNEY FOR PLAINTIFF(S)   JURIS NO.   TELEPHONE NO. (w/area code)

D E F # 1	NAME ADDRESS AND ZIP CODE OF DEFENDANT #1	D E F # 2	NAME ADDRESS AND ZIP CODE OF DEFENDANT #2
	TELEPHONE NO. (w/area code) ("X" ONE) ☐ LLC ☐ PARTNERSHIP ☐ INDIVIDUAL ☐ CORPORATION		TELEPHONE NO. (w/area code) ("X" ONE) ☐ LLC ☐ PARTNERSHIP ☐ INDIVIDUAL ☐ CORPORATION

FOR COURT USE ONLY: ATTORNEY FOR DEFENDANT(S)   JURIS NO.   TELEPHONE NO. (w/area code)

YOU ARE BEING SUED.

THE ABOVE PLAINTIFF(S) **CLAIMS YOU OWE**
PLUS COURT COSTS, FOR THE FOLLOWING REASONS:

AMOUNT DUE

TOWN WHERE TRANSACTION/INJURY OCCURRED OR PREMISES LOCATED

The undersigned, being duly sworn, deposes and says that the signer has read the claim and, to the best of the signer's knowledge, information and belief, there is good ground to support it.

SIGNED
X

TYPE IN NAME AND TITLE OF PERSON SIGNING AT LEFT

SUBSCRIBED AND SWORN TO BEFORE ME ON (Date)

SIGNED (Clerk, Notary, Comm. of Sup. Ct.)
X

The undersigned deposes and says: MILITARY SERVICE AFFIDAVIT

☐ that the undersigned is unable to determine whether or not the defendant(s) in this action are in the military or naval service of the United States.

☐ that the defendant is in the military or naval service of the United States.

☐ that no defendant in this action is in the military or naval service of the United States, and that, to the personal knowledge of the undersigned (state facts showing defendant is not in such service)

FOR COURT USE ONLY
DATE ENTERED

DOCKET NO.

SIGNATURE AND TITLE   X

SUBSCRIBED AND SWORN TO BEFORE ME ON (Date)

SIGNED (Clerk, Notary, Comm. of Sup. Ct.)
X

SIGNED (Clerk)
X

DISTRIBUTION: ORIGINAL - Court   COPY 1- Defendant   COPY 2 - Defendant   COPY 3 - Plaintiff   *www.jud.state.ct.us*

SMALL CLAIMS WRIT AND NOTICE OF SUIT

INSTRUCTIONS TO DEFENDANT

For additional information obtain a copy of "THE SMALL CLAIMS PROCESS" (form JD-CV-45P) from the Clerk's Office

WHAT DO I HAVE TO DO TO DEFEND THIS CASE?
The first and most important step you must take is to file an answer on or BEFORE THE ANSWER DATE. The answer is your statement or reply to the claim stated on this notice. Your reply should be brief but specific. You do not need an attorney even if the plaintiff has one. However, you can have an attorney if you want to hire one. If you want the benefit of the regular rules or if you want the right to appeal this case, you must ask to transfer the case to the regular civil or housing docket. You may need an attorney to assist you and you will have to pay additional fees when you file the motion to transfer the case. The motion to transfer must be filed, in writing, with an affidavit and fees, ON OR BEFORE THE ANSWER DATE.

**WHAT SHOULD I DO IF THE PLAINTIFF
OWES ME MONEY?**
Briefly state how much the plaintiff owes you and why. This portion of your answer is a counterclaim.

WHAT HAPPENS IF I DO NOT FILE AN ANSWER?
If you do not file an answer it means that 1) you do not disagree with the reasons why the plaintiff claims you owe the money AND 2) you do not disagree with the amount of money that the plaintiff claimed. Therefore, if you do not file an answer, the court may enter a judgment against you by default for the full amount of the claim plus court costs.

WHAT IF I KNOW I OWE THE PLAINTIFF SOME MONEY?
Even if you think you owe the plaintiff something, but you disagree with the amount claimed or you are not sure how much you owe the plaintiff, you should file a written answer. This gives you a chance to come to court for a hearing to question how the plaintiff arrived at the amount claimed.

**WHAT SHOULD I DO IF I ADMIT THAT I OWE
THE PLAINTIFF THE ENTIRE AMOUNT CLAIMED?**
1. If you pay the plaintiff/plaintiff's attorney the total amount owed plus court costs, if any, before the answer date, notify the court, on the answer form, that payment has been made. Do not sent payments(s) to the court.

2. If you are sure that you owe the entire amount claimed but you want time to pay, you must file an answer NOT LATER THAN THE ANSWER DATE, stating that you wish time to pay the debt and your reasons for requesting additional time. You may also want to propose a payment schedule.

WHERE AND WHEN DO I HAVE TO GO TO COURT?
After the court receives your answer, it will determine if a hearing is required. YOU DO NOT HAVE TO GO TO COURT ON THE ANSWER DATE but you must make sure the Small Claims Clerk receives your written answer by that date. You will receive a notice of the date, time, and court location of the hearing, if required.

Even if you filed an answer or a request for time to pay, the court can enter a judgment against you if you fail to come to court on the date and time set for a hearing.

**WHAT WILL HAPPEN ON THE DAY
I HAVE TO GO TO COURT?**
1. On the day you are scheduled to be in court, you should get there before the scheduled time.
2. Each case will be called to make sure all the parties are there.
3. The plaintiff's case will be presented first. When the plaintiff has finished you will be given an opportunity to ask questions about the testimony or evidence and then you will be asked
   to present your side of the case. When you are finished, the plaintiff will have an opportunity to ask questions of you and your witnesses.
4. On the day of the hearing, it is essential that you bring all your witnesses and papers, (bills, invoices, checks, etc.) to court with you. This includes any defective or damaged goods that can conveniently be brought to court, estimates of damages, pictures, etc.
5. You should notify your witnesses as soon as you know the hearing date. You may go to the clerk's office to request a subpoena for the witnesses to come to court. There is no fee for the subpoena, but you will have to pay the fee for having it served by a proper officer. This subpoena must be served at least 18 hours before the hearing date unless the court orders otherwise.
6. It might be helpful to make a brief outline of your case for your own use. Although the small claims procedures are designed to be informal, a clear presentation of your position is most important. Although it varies a great deal, you should assume you will be in court a minimum of one to four hours.
7. You will receive a written notice of the court's decision.

WHAT IF I NEED TO POSTPONE THE CASE?
If it is impossible for you to come to court on the day assigned, you should first call the plaintiff or the attorney, if the plaintiff has one, and explain the problem. If the person you called is willing to postpone the case, you should then call the small claims clerk and ask for a continuance and tell the clerk that the plaintiff or the plaintiff's attorney has agreed. Ask the plaintiff or attorney to call the court to confirm the agreement. The clerk will set a new hearing date and send a notice to all parties.

If the plaintiff objects to a continuance, you should still call the clerk, explain your reasons for the request and tell the clerk that the plaintiff does not agree.

Each party will be allowed one continuance if by agreement. Any other requests for a continuance will be referred to the court.

WHAT HAPPENS IF I LOSE THE CASE?
If you lose this case, the court will send you a notice of judgment stating the amount you owe and when it is due. The court may order you to pay the entire amount at one time or to make periodic payments until the entire amount is paid.

WHAT HAPPENS IF I DON'T PAY THE JUDGMENT?
If you fail to make the payment or payments as required, the plaintiff will be entitled to obtain an execution on your wages, bank account or your property. An execution gives a proper officer the authority to attempt to recover the money from your wages, bank account or other property. The plaintiff is also entitled to postjudgment interest and other statutory fees. After the proper officer serves an execution, you will be advised about possible exemption or modification claims that may be available to you.

JD-CV-40, Defendant Rev. 4-01

INSTRUCTIONS TO DEFENDANT

For additional information obtain a copy of "THE SMALL CLAIMS PROCESS" (form JD-CV-45P) from the Clerk's Office

WHAT DO I HAVE TO DO TO DEFEND THIS CASE?
The first and most important step you must take is to file an answer on or BEFORE THE ANSWER DATE. The answer is your statement or reply to the claim stated on this notice. Your reply should be brief but specific. You do not need an attorney even if the plaintiff has one. However, you can have an attorney if you want to hire one. If you want the benefit of the regular rules or if you want the right to appeal this case, you must ask to transfer the case to the regular civil or housing docket. You may need an attorney to assist you and you will have to pay additional fees when you file the motion to transfer the case. The motion to transfer must be filed, in writing, with an affidavit and fees, ON OR BEFORE THE ANSWER DATE.

WHAT SHOULD I DO IF THE PLAINTIFF OWES ME MONEY?
Briefly state how much the plaintiff owes you and why. This portion of your answer is a counterclaim.

WHAT HAPPENS IF I DO NOT FILE AN ANSWER?
If you do not file an answer it means that 1) you do not disagree with the reasons why the plaintiff claims you owe the money AND 2) you do not disagree with the amount of money that the plaintiff claimed. Therefore, if you do not file an answer, the court may enter a judgment against you by default for the full amount of the claim plus court costs.

WHAT IF I KNOW I OWE THE PLAINTIFF SOME MONEY?
Even if you think you owe the plaintiff something, but you disagree with the amount claimed or you are not sure how much you owe the plaintiff, you should file a written answer. This gives you a chance to come to court for a hearing to question how the plaintiff arrived at the amount claimed.

WHAT SHOULD I DO IF I ADMIT THAT I OWE THE PLAINTIFF THE ENTIRE AMOUNT CLAIMED?
1. If you pay the plaintiff/plaintiff's attorney the total amount owed plus court costs, if any, before the answer date, notify the court, on the answer form, that payment has been made. Do not sent payments(s) to the court.

2. If you are sure that you owe the entire amount claimed but you want time to pay, you must file an answer NOT LATER THAN THE ANSWER DATE, stating that you wish time to pay the debt and your reasons for requesting additional time. You may also want to propose a payment schedule.

WHERE AND WHEN DO I HAVE TO GO TO COURT?
After the court receives your answer, it will determine if a hearing is required. YOU DO NOT HAVE TO GO TO COURT ON THE ANSWER DATE but you must make sure the Small Claims Clerk receives your written answer by that date. You will receive a notice of the date, time, and court location of the hearing, if required.

Even if you filed an answer or a request for time to pay, the court can enter a judgment against you if you fail to come to court on the date and time set for a hearing.

WHAT WILL HAPPEN ON THE DAY I HAVE TO GO TO COURT?
1. On the day you are scheduled to be in court, you should get there before the scheduled time.
2. Each case will be called to make sure all the parties are there.
3. The plaintiff's case will be presented first. When the plaintiff has finished you will be given an opportunity to ask questions about the testimony or evidence and then you will be asked to present your side of the case. When you are finished, the plaintiff will have an opportunity to ask questions of you and your witnesses.
4. On the day of the hearing, it is essential that you bring all your witnesses and papers, (bills, invoices, checks, etc.) to court with you. This includes any defective or damaged goods that can conveniently be brought to court, estimates of damages, pictures, etc.
5. You should notify your witnesses as soon as you know the hearing date. You may go to the clerk's office to request a subpoena for the witnesses to come to court. There is no fee for the subpoena, but you will have to pay the fee for having it served by a proper officer. This subpoena must be served at least 18 hours before the hearing date unless the court orders otherwise.
6. It might be helpful to make a brief outline of your case for your own use. Although the small claims procedures are designed to be informal, a clear presentation of your position is most important. Although it varies a great deal, you should assume you will be in court a minimum of one to four hours.
7. You will receive a written notice of the court's decision.

WHAT IF I NEED TO POSTPONE THE CASE?
If it is impossible for you to come to court on the day assigned, you should first call the plaintiff or the attorney, if the plaintiff has one, and explain the problem. If the person you called is willing to postpone the case, you should then call the small claims clerk and ask for a continuance and tell the clerk that the plaintiff or the plaintiff's attorney has agreed. Ask the plaintiff or attorney to call the court to confirm the agreement. The clerk will set a new hearing date and send a notice to all parties.

If the plaintiff objects to a continuance, you should still call the clerk, explain your reasons for the request and tell the clerk that the plaintiff does not agree.

Each party will be allowed one continuance if by agreement. Any other requests for a continuance will be referred to the court.

WHAT HAPPENS IF I LOSE THE CASE?
If you lose this case, the court will send you a notice of judgment stating the amount you owe and when it is due. The court may order you to pay the entire amount at one time or to make periodic payments until the entire amount is paid.

WHAT HAPPENS IF I DON'T PAY THE JUDGMENT?
If you fail to make the payment or payments as required, the plaintiff will be entitled to obtain an execution on your wages, bank account or your property. An execution gives a proper officer the authority to attempt to recover the money from your wages, bank account or other property. The plaintiff is also entitled to postjudgment interest and other statutory fees. After the proper officer serves an execution, you will be advised about possible exemption or modification claims that may be available to you.

JD-CV-40, Defendant Rev. 4-01

INSTRUCTIONS TO PLAINTIFF

For additional information obtain a copy of "THE SMALL CLAIMS PROCESS" (form JD-CV-45P) from the Clerk's Office.

ARE THERE ADDITIONAL EXPENSES INVOLVED?
If the notice of suit is returned to the court undelivered, the clerk shall, upon your request, issue a further notice setting a new answer date. You will have to have a proper officer deliver the court papers, and the proper officer will charge you a fee for the service. When serving an out-of-state corporation, a proper officer must serve the papers and you must pay for the service. If you win the case, you are entitled to recover costs from the defendant. Other expenses, such as service of subpoenas and application fees for execution are also possible. If proper officer's service is not made on the defendant within 120 days from the original answer date, your case may be dismissed.

WHAT HAPPENS IF THE CASE IS TRANSFERRED TO THE REGULAR DOCKET?
If your case is transferred at the defendant's request, the clerk will inform you of that fact. It will be more difficult for you to handle your case without an attorney under the normal court rules. You may wish to consult an attorney.

WHAT HAPPENS AFTER I FILE THE CLAIM?
After you file the claim, the clerk assigns a date by which the defendant has to respond to your claim (this is called the ANSWER DATE) and mails a copy to you and to the defendant. If the defendant does not send an answer to the court by the answer date, a default judgment will enter or a hearing will be scheduled, as appropriate. If the clerk receives an answer from the defendant and your claim is being contested, a hearing will be scheduled. The clerk will send you a copy of the defendant's answer. You and the defendant will receive a written notice from the court telling you when to come to court. If the defendant files a counterclaim against you, you must file an answer to the counterclaim by the new answer date which will be assigned.

WHAT IF I NEED TO POSTPONE THE CASE?
If it is impossible for you to come to court on the day assigned, you should first call the defendant or the attorney, if the defendant has one, and explain the problem. If the person you called is willing to postpone the case, you should then call the small claims clerk and ask for a continuance and tell the clerk that the defendant or the defendant's attorney has agreed. Ask the defendant or attorney to call the court to confirm the agreement. The clerk will set a new hearing date and send a notice to all parties. If the defendant objects to a continuance, you should still call the clerk, explain your reasons for the request and tell the clerk that the defendant does not agree.

Each party will be allowed one continuance if by agreement. Any other requests for a continuance will be referred to the court. However, during the months of January and July of each year, small claims cases which have not gone to judgment within one year from the date on which they were filed shall be dismissed.

WHAT WILL HAPPEN ON THE DAY I HAVE TO GO TO COURT?
1. On the day you are scheduled to be in court, you should get to court before the scheduled time.
2. Each case will be called to make sure all the parties are there.
3. Your case will be presented first. When you have finished, the defendant will be given an opportunity to ask you or your witnesses questions about what has been said or other evidence that has been presented. The defendant will then be asked to tell his or her side of the case. You will be given a similar opportunity to ask questions of the defendant and defendant's witnesses when he or she has finished.
4. You will be advised of the court's decision a few days after the hearing.

HOW SHOULD I PREPARE FOR THE TRIAL?
On the day of the hearing, it is essential that you bring all your witnesses and any papers (bills, leases, invoices, checks, etc.) to court with you. This includes any defective or damaged goods that can be brought to court conveniently, estimates of damage, pictures, etc. You should notify your witnesses as soon as you know the hearing date. You may go to the clerk's office to request a subpoena for the witnesses to come to court. There is no fee to request the subpoena, but you will have to pay the fee to have it served by a proper officer. This subpoena must be served at least 18 hours before the hearing unless the court orders otherwise.

Although it varies a great deal, you should assume you will be in court a minimum of one to four hours. It might be helpful to make a brief outline of your case for your own use. Although the small claims procedures are designed to be informal, a clear presentation of your position is most important.

WHAT HAPPENS IF I WIN THE CASE?
If you win the case the court will send you a notice of the amount owed you and when it is due. If you have asked for and received an order for periodic payments, the notice will specify how much is to be paid to you (or your attorney if you have one) and when the payments are to begin. This decision of the court is called the "judgment."

CAN I APPEAL THIS CASE?
No. If you want to be able to appeal this case, then you must file your claim with the regular civil or housing docket of the Superior Court. If the defendant files a counterclaim to your small claims suit, you may file a motion to transfer the case to the regular civil or housing docket. Cases filed with, or transferred to, the regular civil or housing docket will be more expensive and complicated and you will probably need an attorney, but you will be able to appeal if you lose.

CAN THE DEFENDANT APPEAL IF I WIN?
No. If the defendant wants to be able to appeal, the case must be transferred to the regular civil or housing docket of the Superior Court. Although very few defendants ask to transfer a case, the defendant does have same right to transfer the case. Generally, if the defendant makes his request by the ANSWER DATE, and in the right manner, the judge or magistrate must order the case transferred.

WHAT SHOULD I DO IF THE DEFENDANT DOES NOT PAY THE JUDGMENT?
If the defendant fails to make the payment or payments as required, you are entitled to ask the court for an execution. An execution gives a proper officer the authority to attempt to recover the money on your behalf from the defendant's wages, bank account or other property. The details on how to obtain an execution, if you need one, are explained on the Notice of Judgment you will receive from the court after the case is finished. The most important thing to remember is that the court does not collect the money for you. Rather, the court's purpose is to hear the case and make a decision and to give you the necessary permission to have its orders enforced if they are not complied with.

JD-CV-40, Plaintiff Rev. 4-01

GLOSSARY

Action at Law—A judicial proceeding whereby one party prosecutes another for a wrong done.

Actionable—Giving rise to a cause of action.

Actual Damages—Actual damages are those damages directly referable to the breach or tortious act, and which can be readily proven to have been sustained, and for which the injured party should be compensated as a matter of right.

Adjudicate—When a judge hears and decides a case.

Adjudication—The judge's decision in a case or action.

Admissible Evidence—Evidence that can legally and properly be used in court.

Admission—A statement that certain facts are true.

Adversary System—The system of trial practice in the United States and some other countries in which each of the opposing parties has the opportunity to present and establish opposing positions before the court.

Adverse Witness—A person called to testify for the other side.

Affidavit—A written statement that someone swears to under oath in front of someone that is legally authorized, like a judge or notary public.

Affirm—To make a solemn statement.

Affirmative Defense—In a pleading, a matter constituting a defense.

Allegation—A statement or claim that is made and hasn't been proved to be true or false.

Allege—To state that something is true even though it hasn't yet been proven.

Alternative Dispute Resolution (ADR)—Methods of resolving disputes without official court proceedings, including mediation and arbitration.

Ambient Noise—The all-encompassing noise associated with a given environment, being usually a composite of sounds from many sources near and far.

American Arbitration Association (AAA)—National organization of arbitrators from whose panel arbitrators are selected for labor and civil disputes.

Answer—In a civil proceeding, the principal pleading on the part of the defendant in response to the plaintiff's complaint.

Appearance—To come into court, personally or through an attorney, after being summoned.

Arbitration—A method of resolving a dispute in which a third party renders a decision.

Arbitration Clause—A clause inserted in a contract providing for compulsory arbitration in case of dispute as to the rights or liabilities under such contract.

Arbitrator—A private, disinterested person, chosen by the parties to a disputed question, for the purpose of hearing their contention, and awarding judgment to the prevailing party.

Asset—The entirety of a person's property, either real or personal.

Boundary Line—The dividing line between two adjacent properties.

Burden of Proof—The duty of a party to substantiate an allegation or issue to convince the trier of fact as to the truth of their claim.

Cause of Action—The charges that make up the case or lawsuit.

Civil Action—An action maintained to protect a private, civil right as opposed to a criminal action.

Civil Court—The court designed to resolve disputes arising under the common law and civil statutes.

Civil Law—Law which applies to noncriminal actions.

Circumstantial Evidence—Indirect evidence not based on actual personal knowledge or observation of the facts in dispute.

Clean Hands Doctrine—The concept that claimants who seek equitable relief must not themselves have indulged in any impropriety in relation to the transaction upon which relief is sought.

Complaint—The form that the plaintiff completes and files to begin a lawsuit in a small claims court, a copy of which must be served on the defendant.

Compromise and Settlement—An arrangement arrived at, either in court or out of court, for settling a dispute upon what appears to the parties to be equitable terms.

Conciliation—Conciliation is often used interchangeably with mediation to describe a method of dispute settlement whereby parties clarify issues and narrow differences through the aid of a neutral facilitator.

Consequential Damages—Consequential damages are those damages which are caused by an injury, but which are not a necessary result of the injury, and must be specially pleaded and proven in order to be awarded.

Costs—Certain fees and charges a party pays to file and present a case or to enforce a judgment.

Counterclaim—The part of the response that says why the Plaintiff owes the Defendant money or property.

Court—The branch of government responsible for the resolution of disputes arising under the laws of the government.

Court of Conciliation—A court which proposes terms of adjustment of a dispute so as to avoid litigation.

Cross-claim—A demand by the defendant against the plaintiff. The cross claim is usually heard at the same hearing as the plaintiff's claim. It need not relate to the plaintiff's claim.

Cross-examination—The testimony a witness gives when the opposing side is asking the questions at a trial.

Damages—In general, damages refers to monetary compensation which the law awards to one who has been injured by the actions of another, such as in the case of tortious conduct or breach of contractual obligations.

Defendant—In a civil proceeding, the party responding to the complaint.

Defense—Opposition to the truth or validity of the plaintiff's claims.

Enforce—To put the judgment into effect by taking legal steps to bring about compliance.

Execution—Carrying out some act or course of conduct to its completion. Execution upon a money judgment is the legal process of enforcing the judgment, usually by seizing and selling property of the debtor.

Filing Fees—Money paid to the court clerk to file court papers and start a civil case.

General Damages—General damages are those damages directly referable to the breach or tortious act and which can be readily proven to have been sustained, and for which the injured party should be compensated as a matter of right.

Good Cause—A sufficient reason.

In Rem—Refers to actions that are against property, and concerned with the disposition of that property, rather than against the person.

Injunction—A judicial remedy either requiring a party to perform an act, or restricting a party from continuing a particular act.

Injury—Any damage done to another's person, rights, reputation or property.

Judge—The individual who presides over a court, and whose function it is to determine controversies.

Judgment—A judgment is a final determination by a court of law concerning the rights of the parties to a lawsuit.

Jurisdictional Limit—The maximum monetary amount that may be awarded by a small claims court.

Mediation—A process in which a neutral third person helps the parties in a dispute discuss their problem and work out their own mutually acceptable solution.

Mediation/Arbitration—Combination of mediation and arbitration which utilizes a neutral selected to serve as both mediator and arbitrator in a dispute. The techniques of persuasion and discussion, as used in mediation, are combined with the arbitrator's authority to issues a final and binding decision, when necessary.

Mediation and Conciliation Service—An independent department of the federal government charged with trying to settle labor disputes by conciliation and mediation.

Mediator—A neutral third person who helps disputants arrive at their own settlement. The mediator doesn't decide the dispute.

Minitrial—A confidential, nonbinding exchange of information, intended to facilitate settlement.

Negotiation—The process in which the parties to a dispute communicate their differences to each other, through conference, discussion and compromise, in an attempt to resolve them.

Nominal Damages—A trivial sum of money which is awarded as recognition that a legal injury was sustained, although slight.

Parties—The disputants.

Personal Jurisdiction—The power of a court over the person of a defendant.

Personal Service—Handing a copy of court papers directly to the person to be served.

Plaintiff—The person or entity who files the lawsuit.

Process—Court papers that notify a person that he or she is being sued.

Process Server—A person who serves court papers on a party to a suit.

Proof of Service—A form that must be completed by the person serving court papers on a party, stating that service was properly made.

Property Line—The official dividing line between properties.

Real property—Land and any permanent fixtures on it, including buildings, trees, and other fixtures.

Release—A document signed by one party, releasing claims he or she may have against another party, usually as part of a settlement agreement.

Response—Also referred to as an Answer, Defendant's statement as to why the claim is not true or is inaccurate as to amount.

Restitution—The act of restoring or giving the equivalent value to compensate for an injury, damage, or loss.

Satisfaction—The discharge and release of an obligation.

Service by Publication—When service of process is done by publishing a notice in a newspaper after a court determines that other means of service are impractical or have been unsuccessful.

Service of Process—The delivery of legal court documents, such as a complaint, to the defendant.

Settlement—An agreement by the parties to a dispute on a resolution of the claims, usually requiring some mutual action, such as payment of money in consideration of a release of claims.

Small Claims Court—The division of the trial court that handles civil cases asking for damages below a prescribed limit, e.g., $5,000, which is intended to be more expedient and less costly than a regular civil lawsuit.

Sound Level Meter—Any instrument including a microphone, amplifier, an output meter, and frequency weighting networks for the measurement of noise and sound levels in a specific manner.

Sound Reproduction Device—A device intended primarily for the production or reproduction of sound, including but not limited to any musical instrument, radio receiver, television receiver, tape recorder, phonograph or sound amplifying system.

Statute of Limitations—Any law which fixes the time within which parties must take judicial action to enforce rights or thereafter be barred from enforcing them.

Stay—A judicial order suspending some action until further court order lifting the stay.

Stipulation—An admission or agreement made by parties to a lawsuit concerning the pending matter.

Summons—The portion of the Complaint which informs the Defendant when and where to appear.

Tenancy at Will—The right to occupy property for an indefinite period of time.

Tenant—A person that rents property.

Title—The legal document conferring ownership of a piece of real estate.

Tort—A private or civil wrong.

Tortfeasor—A person that commits or is found guilty of a tort.

Trial—The judicial procedure whereby disputes are determined based on the presentation of issues of law and fact. Issues of fact are decided by the trier of fact, either the judge or jury, and issues of law are decided by the judge.

Trial Court—The court of original jurisdiction over a particular matter.

Trial Date—The date that the Plaintiff and Defendant must appear in Court.

Unconscionable—Refers to a bargain so one-sided as to amount to an absence of meaningful choice on the part of one of the parties, together with terms which are unreasonably favorable to the other party.

Unreasonable Noise—Any excessive or unusually loud sound that disturbs the peace, comfort or repose of a reasonable person of normal sensitivities or injures or endangers the health or safety of a reasonable person of normal sensitivities or which causes injury to plant or animal life, or damage to property or business.

Venue—The particular court in which an action may properly be brought.

Voluntary Arbitration—Arbitration which occurs by mutual and free consent of the parties.

Waive—To abandon or give up a claim or a right.

Zoning—Regulations that control the use of land within a jurisdiction.

BIBLIOGRAPHY AND ADDITIONAL RESOURCES

American Arbitration Association (Date Visited: October 2006) <http:www.adr.org/>.

American Bar Association (Date Visited: October 2006) <http://www.abanet.org/>.

American Society for the Prevention of Cruelty to Animals (Date Visited: October 2006) <http://www.aspca.org/>.

Black's Law Dictionary, Fifth Edition. St. Paul, MN: West Publishing Company, 1979.

Encarta World English Dictionary. New York, NY: St. Martin's Press, 1999.

Insurance Information Institute (Date Visited: October 2006) <http://www.iii.org/>.

International Society of Arboriculture (ISA) (Date Visited: October 2006) http://www.isa-arbor.com/>.

Rhode Island General Laws § 34-10-20.

The Noise Pollution Clearinghouse (NPC) (Date Visited: October 2006) http://www.nonoisel.org/lawlib/cities/cities.htm/>.

The United States Environmental Protection Agency (Date Visited: October 2006) <http://www.epa.gov/>.

Village of Massapequa Zoning Law § 345-40.